DIRTY LITTLE SECRETS

DIRTY LITTLE SECRETS

LOUIS CARR

Seraph Books

www.seraphbooks.com

www.LouisCarrBook.com

www.LouisCarrFoundation.org

By permission. From *Merriam-Webster's Collegiate® Dictionary, 11th Edition* © 2016 by Merriam-Webster, Inc. (www.Merriam-Webster.com).

ISBN Paperback: 978-1-941711-18-7
ISBN Hardcover: 978-1-941711-15-6
Library of Congress Control Number: 2016936639

PRINTED AND BOUND IN THE UNITED STATES OF AMERICA
10 9 8 7 6 5 4 3 2 1

Cover design by Alyssa M. Curry

Copyediting by Alyssa M. Curry

Cover and author photos by Akintayo Adewole
for Adewole Photography, www.adewole.com

For information regarding special discounts for bulk purchases of this book for educational, gift purposes, as a charitable donation, or to arrange a speaking event, please visit: www.seraphbooks.com

To my wife, Diane. Thank you so much for your love, patience, and support. What a ride it has been. I look forward to the next thirty years! I love you.

Information has value, which is the reason many people are disinclined to share. Instead, they selfishly protect their experiences and paths to success as though they are patented, dirty little secrets. In essence, they have no desire to offer you the advantage to achieve what they may or may not have.

CONTENTS

CONTENTS

FOREWORD

There are great secrets in my longtime friend and former colleague's book *Dirty Little Secrets*, however certainly not dirty ones. What is in abundance in this book by BET's President of Media Sales, Louis Carr, is page after page of life-affirming wisdom and spiritual inspiration. Most of all, what you will gain from reading this book is an introduction of life lessons that Louis has learned and mastered based on his indomitable intellect, a personal character rooted in faith, and his emotional self-commitment to make people's lives better.

You will be motivated and inspired by Louis' life and his firm belief that the challenges we confront in work and life can be overcome by faith, perseverance, and the pursuit of perfection.

I hired Louis on August 11, 1986, to help me build and lead our advertising sales department at Black Entertainment Television (BET). Little did I know at the time that I had discovered a "wunderkind" who by his will, determination, and zeal to maximize his God-given talents, was destined to become the most significant contributor, then and now, to the financial success of BET.

This book, *Dirty Little Secrets*, is Louis' way of paying forward enlightened and beneficial knowledge to all who choose to read and immerse themselves in the lessons in this book—and I hope that is everyone.

Louis can best be described as a businessman's humanitarian. After reading his book, you will be inspired and uplifted. I was so inspired, I chose this quote from one of my favorite books, which, for me, defines Louis' message: "What is a good man, but a bad man's teacher? What is a bad man, but a good man's job? If you don't understand this, you will get lost, however intelligent you are. It is the great secret." Louis Carr has discovered it for you. Please enjoy his wonderful book of secrets for life.

Bob Johnson, Founder
Black Entertainment Television and The RLJ Companies

DIRTY LITTLE SECRETS

INTRODUCTION

As we move forward on our individual journey through life, we will encounter numerous goals we want to achieve and then come to the realization that there are tasks we are meant to achieve. Our journey will introduce us to many types of individuals, some of whom will impact our life in the most profound way, selflessly pouring insights into us. These are the individuals who will teach us our most valuable lessons. Some of those lessons we may understand as they unfold, while others are certain to take time. However, when we pause to give reflection to our achievements, it will become transparent we gained the proper appreciation and wisdom during our journey.

I began my life never feeling there was anything special about me. I didn't believe I possessed any particular qualities to make me somewhat different from those around me. But for some reason, people who were close to me always perceived there to be something more in me than what I saw in myself. As time went on, others often acknowledged that same perspective; causing me to accept there was something worth cultivating that could prove them right. Believing that special something would become discernible when it was time, I had to be willing to take my journey with faith.

Although that revelation didn't occur until I was a sophomore in high school, I've known for many years that where I am in life was always a part of my destiny. Once I accepted that I had something special, it began to manifest inside of me. There is something special waiting for you to acknowledge in your life so that you can take action. The only way you will reach your destiny is to stay the course, regardless of the challenges that may come.

Information has value, which is the reason many people are disinclined to share. Instead, they selfishly protect their experiences and paths to success as though they are patented, dirty little secrets. In essence, they have no desire to offer you the advantage to achieve what they may or may not have. Unfortunately, you will meet people who prefer that you encounter the same struggles they've endured. However, it is my intent to share the lessons that have helped me excel in business and my personal life. Some are rarely spoken of, yet they are relatable and critical aspects that will assist in helping you understand and find the correct path to your destiny, just as I have done. I am not claiming it will be easy, but I am assuring you that with hard work, focus, and a willingness to learn, it can be done.

I consider *Dirty Little Secrets* as sort of a payment on the debt I owe to everyone who has helped me get here; and that list began when I was a child. It is comprised of parents, relatives, teachers, coaches, neighbors, professors, and anyone in my memory bank that contributed to my personal growth and success.

It was hard for me to understand how people believed I could be better than I thought I could be, but they did. When you are raised in a poor situation, you have the propensity to become a part of that environment, which makes it hard to envision much beyond those invisible barriers. Without vision, it's difficult to imagine there is anything more or that you need anything else.

As I progressed through various stages of my life, success came into view. I began my career in media as an Account Executive, advancing through the many levels of management. Over thirty-four years, I was promoted from a Director to a VP, SVP, EVP, and then President. There was a wealth of information and crucial layers of comprehension that came with each of those positions. They required a different type of skill set based on the task and the environment at that time. Although I've been in the media industry for over thirty-four years, I never imagined that I would have tenure with *one* company for over thirty years. The information that I am sharing with you is the key to my success.

Converging with time, success ultimately came to fruition in many ways. Through experience and self-reflection, I understood the reason I didn't see anything special about myself was because I didn't have vision. The lack of vision will impede your progress and keep you from your destiny as it began to do with me. Without vision, it is impossible to see your blessings.

I believe there was a plan laid down before the foundation of the world and that people are placed in our lives for different reasons, which are not accidents nor happenstance. The things I have been through were instrumental in preparing me for this stage of my life, and I am so appreciative for my journey. I have a destiny, and you have a destiny that was preordained by God. I believe that faith is one of the most crucial aspects as to whether or not we will reach our intended destiny. I want you to challenge yourself to determine how you will reach yours.

{1}

3:19:5

Time: the thing that is measured as seconds, minutes, hours, days, years, etc.

Each of us has a particular path that will lead us somewhere, and where we end up is predicated on whether or not we pay attention to the path we have chosen. Growing up on the West Side of Chicago, my mother and grandmother made sure I stayed on one particular course until I reached a point where I could understand my journey. It's not an effortless undertaking to keep children on the right path, but the way they accomplished it was by raising me under a disciplined structure. Their structure taught me how to force myself to focus without the excuse of distractions. As a result, I became committed to any goal I established, which facilitated my ability to achieve respectable grades in diverse educational environments. I was acceptant of others who were different and followed instructions. And when it came to trouble, I stayed out of it—*most of the time.*

Initially, I wasn't interested in participating in many of the activities other kids enjoyed; so I spent a great deal of time alone. But in time, that changed. I played most sports, including football, until I broke my arm. Since some of my friends ran track, I hung out at their practices and naturally started running with them while my cast was still on. It didn't take long before the coach asked me to join the team.

My mother, grandmother, relatives, teachers, and others had always insisted that I was special. Although I'd done well in school and other areas, at the time, I didn't believe I was that guy. It wasn't until we started racking up wins during my sophomore and junior years at Lane Technical High School that something began to manifest inside of me. It seemed that my track coach sensed something, too.

One afternoon, my coach started screaming at me. He took the baton and drew a line in the cinder track. "Louis, make a decision. Are you going to be great or are you going to be just good?" he said, pointing to each side of the line with the baton.

"What's the difference? What do the people do who are great versus the people who are good?"

"You've answered my question by asking me that question. Line up!" he instructed. He didn't have to say anything else; he'd made his point. I focused and worked even harder *to be great.*

After the team won city indoor and outdoor championships both years, the coaches claimed that I was special, too. It finally started to resonate with me once the *Chicago Tribune* and the *Chicago Sun-Times* began writing about me. Finally, I conceded and made the decision to stop fighting it. I pushed harder to get the mechanics down to a science so that I could improve and own that blessing.

During my junior and senior years, conversations about scholarship offers developed. I didn't know of anyone, other than my cousin Rodney, who had gone to college; so the idea of pursuing an undergraduate degree wasn't on my radar. Instinctively, I wanted to emulate the people around me who worked hard and wore uniforms. Besides, I was extremely close to my mother and grandmother; so life was good. And evident by the bond and level of respect we displayed for one another, the guys on the track team were family, too. We were always together. As a result, I didn't know how I felt about college since it wasn't a part of what I knew. The conversation alone placed me in an uncomfortable space.

Committed to accomplishing my goals, I trained year-round. During the summer of my sophomore and junior years, I ran for the Chicago Zephyrs Track Club and was coached by the founder of the track club, Jane Dickens, and three-time Olympic Gold Medalist Wilma Rudolph.

That experience was invaluable. It's where my preparation to become a great sprinter occurred, and my foundation was being custom built with reinforcements. While having fun, I worked on the mechanics and fundamentals of sprinting. Quickly identifying my deficiencies, Wilma Rudolph taught me how to run with my hips up and chest out in a straight position instead of crouching down. One of the most valuable lessons began with learning how to maintain proper form when I had those last few yards to go. My shoulders unconsciously went up when I grew tired; so she taught me the correct form. After that, we worked on the way my body and mind would react when I became exhausted. Being a good student, I learned to trust the person giving direction and respectfully did what I was told. Wilma Rudolph said, "Regardless of how tired you are, don't fall apart." I was certain her advice would be an essential component to winning.

The track team wanted to win so badly we went to the extent of practicing with the cross-country team in the fall. Although running several miles was a struggle, we did it to further prepare ourselves for the indoor and outdoor track seasons. Over the holidays, we practiced at the University of Chicago's Field House to make sure we were at our best. Since track meets began the second week of January, we had to be ready for competition; therefore, taking a break never reached my mindset.

When I returned to school my senior year, I was

seventeen and captain of the track team. I could tell something was ignited in me that I couldn't disregard. Track had become a lifestyle, causing me to have a vision of accomplishing something greater than winning. That September, I wrote down on a piece of paper the time I believed we could achieve in the mile relay and taped it to the inside of my locker. That time was 3:19:5.

When I showed my coach, Barney McCall, his reply was, "Yeah. Y'all are good, but you ain't that good, son. That's never gonna happen."

My eyebrows quickly arched together as I contemplated the validity of his words. *He didn't tell me that's not gonna happen, did he?* I thought, refusing to accept his opinion. *I think that can happen,* I added, affirming that it was possible. Once I had the vision of running 3:19:5, it never left me because I claimed it even before I'd spoken it. I told the guys on the relay team I believed we could break the world record. At first, they laughed, but it didn't matter because I kept pushing our coach to believe that we could do it. The more I spoke it into existence, the more they began to believe it, too. Finally, Coach McCall said, "Well, let's map it out. Let's see what time each leg would have to run to do this 3:19:5."

We went at it, even battling one another in practice. And although many tried, I was unwilling to allow anyone to outwork me, especially after my mother and grandmother often lectured me about working hard. I watched films, practiced my form in the mirror, and focused on getting the mechanics down. By the time I stepped onto the track, it was already ingrained. I was an unyielding competitor when it came to working harder and longer than anyone else. I was certain that if I wanted to be successful, I had to be all in, all the time.

All in, all the time means you are committed to a goal, vision, or plan all the time.

As a whole, our team had achieved a significant level of success on the track. With all the time and work invested, instinctively we learned to trust one another because we knew the skill set and capabilities of each other well. Continuously taught the value of hard work, I decided if that was all I had to do to be successful, it would happen.

Separating the men from the boys, one of the hardest workouts I ever did were the forty-second runs. Given enough time for a full recovery in between all three, we sprinted all-out with the goal of going farther each time. If we went two hundred and eighty yards the first time, we pushed to go three hundred the second attempt, and then three hundred and thirty, working to build endurance during the process. Strategically, Coach McCall never put the four of us together with the intent of creating a natural competition. Each of us ran with a different group of sprinters and I always heard Coach yelling for us to push through it. After the last run, we were eager to find out how far the others had gone. The constant development of our fighting spirit facilitated an ultimate respect for talent amongst us. If one of us had an off day, no one complained. Instead, the other three made up the time. With every meet, we came closer and closer, knowing that 3:19:5 was within reach.

Coach emphasized that people who are great are willing to put forth more effort versus those who are good. At that age, hard work taught me everything; I knew what I wanted to be. When he said, "Know you're tired, but force yourself through it. Lean into it and commit to the hard work," I did. Subsequently, doing the cool-downs and stretching was fundamental to the process, even though I hated it.

I attended one of the biggest high schools in the state. Lane Tech was built to hold over ten thousand students, although at that time, it only had approximately five thousand. The environment and the facilities they offered made a difference in the way I learned. The setting was similar to a college campus. The ceilings were high and the hallways were wide. There was nothing small or normal about the size of this school. Built on thirty-three beautiful acres, Lane Tech required high academic standards for admission.

There were over one hundred kids on the track team

and a large coaching staff because several of our teachers volunteered. It seemed as though everyone wanted to be part of a successful team. When Lane Tech walked into a building, we made a statement because the entire team traveled to the meets.

To alleviate any surprises the night before a meet, the coaches had us mentally prepare by walking the race, mapping it out, and taking in the essence of the environment. We made sure we knew the curves and understood what we were going to do for each part of the race. They would ask, "What do you see now? How do you feel? What do you see on the backstretch?" forcing a powerful mental connection, which allowed my mind to create the visual of the race. Once I saw it, I could feel it.

The last week in March 1974, our team entered the University of Chicago Field House in Hyde Park blasting our theme song, "I'll Take You There" by The Staple Singers. With standing room only, it was the biggest crowd I had ever seen in that building. The strong menthol smell slipped up my nostrils as I caught sight of the Harlem Cheerleaders exciting the crowd in their powder blue and white uniforms. Lane Tech had a rivalry with Wendell Philips Academy High School and the anticipation of an incredible outcome filtered heavily, adding heat to the atmosphere. The crowd expected to witness something special that night. Dressed in our green and gold sweats, Kevin Newell, Dennis Kern, Tim Klein, and I warmed up together. We stretched, ran our wind sprints, and pumped each other up. However, the swagger I typically carried was subdued; I wasn't myself.

———————◆———————

Track is a team sport based on individual performance to achieve a team goal.

———————◆———————

Before the race started, we had our individual routines. I walked off to be by myself. I needed to pray and eliminate distractions until I accomplished my objective. Concentrating and being in the moment before the race was critical. It allowed me to remove everything from my mind so I could focus on that one thing I had to execute. Training for the 440 taught me how to stay in the moment longer than most and I was prepared to do so.

It was so crowded that the only place to warm up was where the field events were held, and that wasn't the safest place. Attempting to stay loose until the relay, I sat in the bleachers with Kevin. Stretching out my right leg, I turned my foot from side-to-side, and something in my hamstring made a loud clicking sound. A strange sensation kicked up high near my butt, like something was loose. A wave of concern spread across Kevin's face and he said, "That ain't good." He was right, but I didn't have time to think about anything else because there was too much on the line. Kevin studied my eyes as if the reflection he usually saw was somehow different. He could see the determination while sensing the hunger inside of me because he had it, too.

Winning is having the right to decide when you're going to stop. My drive and commitment to breaking that record wouldn't allow it. Regardless, I was scared and certain the mile relay would be exceedingly difficult, hurting more than it ever had before. I had never faced a challenge where winning wasn't the end. This time, I believed we could break the world record. It was set back in 1920 by Boys High School in New York. The only thing I owned that night was the fear of not being successful.

When it was time for the race, I watched Kevin position himself in the blocks with calculated precision. When the gun sounded, he shot out, accelerating into a sprint with everything he had in him. When he hit the exchange zone, he handed a blind pass to Dennis with a solid lead in first place. After extending the lead, he ended with a flawless blind handoff to our third leg, Tim. Wendell Phillips put the second-best quarter-miler on their team against Tim, who closed the gap, adding to the tension. I knew Hatch, one of the best quarter-milers in the state, was the anchor for Wendell Phillips. When Tim hit the zone, I turned, began running, and extended my arm to receive a perfect blind pass of the baton in first place, a yard ahead of Wendell Phillips. Completely focused, I took off. With every calculated step, my mind and body were in sync as I forced myself to sprint harder than I ever considered possible. I kept telling myself, *Relax, stay in control, keep your knees up, and pump your arms.* I did exactly what the forty-second runs taught me. If I needed to respond with a different type of gear, I wanted to be able to do that.

By the time we reached the last curve, Wendell Phillips was right on my shoulder, pressing hard with every single step. For a fleeting moment, the track led us behind the bleachers, taking us out of view. When we reappeared, I had the lead on Hatch and kept it up the final straightaway. In my black and red Adidas, I depleted everything I had in me as I leaned across the finish line five or six yards ahead of him. And then, I ceased to the sound of Coach Lewis calling off the time, 3:19:5—and we lost it! A deafening sound of excitement rocked the Field House as the crowd went wild. Not only had we won the City Championship, but we'd also broken the indoor National Interscholastic Record and High School World Record in the mile relay! *Teamwork makes a dream work.*

The impact that 3:19:5 had on us in regard to being disciplined, focused, working hard, operating as a team, and setting goals prepared each of us for our life journey. Every curve and straightaway that night helped shape the men we would become. We were known as the Fearsome Foursome.

{2}

DEFEATING ADVERSITY

---

*Adversity: a state or instance of serious or
continued difficulty or misfortune*

The morning of March 30th, I was still on a high
from the night before, when we had broken the high
school world record. In preparation for the Oak Park
Relays, I could tell the muscle in my right leg didn't feel
normal, but in spite of that, I worked through it. It hadn't
prevented us from setting a world record, so I let it go. I
ran a total of twenty-one events that week, including pre-
liminaries and finals. Still feeling a constant twinge, my
muscles were tired, but I warmed them up well.

Our team was known for having the fundamentals down to an undeviating exactitude. We were able
to get out of the blocks with precision, maintain proper
form, accelerate to an impressive speed, and deliver the

best blind baton exchange possible. Indisputably, we had exceptional coaching.

Kevin Newell won his heat of the 50 and my heat was next. My pedals were adjusted farther apart than most sprinters', causing my first step to be more comfortable since I was strong and had a long stride. I considered myself average when it came to talent, but what I did have was God-given insight. I understood precisely what I needed to do to be exceptionally competitive.

Muscular but lean at one hundred and seventy pounds, I stood in front of my blocks until I heard "Runners take your mark!" At that instruction, I came down in a squat, placing my hands out in front of me. Crawling backward, beginning with my left leg, I placed my foot on the pedal followed by my right foot. The clicking was still there. I sat with my upper body straight up and looked forward until I heard "Set!" Then, I rolled up into a motionless stance. When the gun sounded, with a powerful thrust, my left arm drove forward simultaneously with my first few steps, activating my rhythm. If you are not in rhythm, you can have difficulties because you are not hitting all cylinders. Having extremely high knee lifts, when my right leg went up, I could feel it disrupting my focus. I thought to myself, *This is not good.* By the time I was thirty yards out, there was a loud pop. I reached back, clutching my right hamstring. The pain was so intense I went down yelling. Coach McCall raced toward me vehemently instructing, "Don't try to move! Don't try to move!" And then he started to curse while I grimaced in pain. I will never forget the look of concern that flushed across his face while his eyes welled with an inaudible alert, telling me it was bad. And I'm certain my expression indicated I'd never had that type of excruciating pain burning in the back of my hamstring driving up through my butt. They rushed to put ice on it and shortly afterward took me to be evaluated by the physical therapist for the Chicago Blackhawks. Nothing could have prepared me for being told, "Your career is over. You will be lucky if you don't walk without a limp."

Take an account of the reality by obtaining an understanding of what happened, how the situation happened, and why.

When facing adversity, the natural human instinct is to give in. Time and again, you won't see it coming; therefore, adversity can hit you like a hammer in the back of the head. It has a shock-and-awe effect, and it is surprising—in a bad way. The first thing you should do when you meet adversity is regroup. Take an account of the reality by obtaining an understanding of what happened, how the situation happened, and why. Then, devise a plan on how you will defeat adversity, taking into consideration that a significant change may need to occur.

Whether it is losing weight, changing jobs, or moving to a different neighborhood, change can be difficult. Even when it's for the better, change isn't easy. It has its share of uncertainty, which is why preparation is necessary. Once you have accurately assessed the situation, implement a plan that addresses where you are and how you will come through it. In order to get out of that uncomfortable place, attach a timeline to create a sense of urgency.

Just as there is sunshine, there is rain; and I look at God's Word as an umbrella that is going to protect me.

Since adversity has the ability to catch you off guard, it will deplete your energy. You have to be able to create the fire or energy to motivate yourself. It will be necessary when facing a difficult challenge.

Regardless of how busy I am in my career or how often I travel, I have always tried to prepare for adversity by going to church and learning God's Word on a regular basis. Just as there is sunshine, there is rain; and I look at God's Word as an umbrella that is going to protect me from inclement weather. Sometimes, I have to go through the storm, but I'm not worried because it's not going to drown me. God's umbrella will keep me from getting too wet.

During my journey, I have learned lessons that are applicable, even today.

- At some point in time, adversity is going to be right around the corner. And it is usually at the *best* of times.

- Just because you face it once or twice, doesn't mean it won't happen again.

- A common mistake is to underestimate the power of God's Word. The Bible is filled with one critical account after another with examples of how people pushed through many forms of adversity.

- In your darkest moments, the Word can inspire you.

When something hits you so hard it throws you off balance physically, emotionally, or mentally, the best way to prepare for combat is through prayer. Prayer is calming and therapeutic to the mind. It can remove stress and doubt from a mindset filled with negativity. Prayer will help you sustain both your faith and strength so you can push through and ultimately defeat adversity.

The ability to take from life rather than investing in it is common, but you will learn that taking without giving is detrimental to the process of creating value. Friendship is one example of this. It is important to build a strong foundational network of friends and people who have a positive attitude. When adversity arrives at your door, you will have a support group that can help push you through any situation that arises. You don't want to be around people who haven't been successful when it comes to defeating adversity.

All of us require something that is bigger than ourselves, which is why I believe faith is important. We can do everything we know possible, but most of the time, we need God to do the rest. Some people will fervently state that they don't want to hear about "that religious stuff" or "that faith stuff." What it reveals is they haven't been low enough, yet. Faith offers more than anyone can give you and I am afraid of anyone who doesn't have it.

Remember, when adversity arrives, you will need something greater than yourself to defeat it. Therefore, you must not be afraid to admit you need help from a greater place. A part of understanding your journey is accepting that adversity contributes to your growth. Just make sure you have a mental picture of what you're going to look like when you get through it—and come out on the other side.

{3}

BLESSINGS AND MIRACLES

Blessing: a thing conducive to happiness or welfare

We have the tendency to take a great deal for granted and the many blessings we receive are examples. A blessing is something that is more than you can work to achieve. It is the extra that is poured on top of your faith and the work that you have done. It will surprise you and bring happiness.

Just as there are blessings, there are miracles. Miracles are extraordinary events that go beyond human comprehension, such as Peter walking on water in the Bible. Even the most creative mind could not have imagined that possibility as miracles are without boundaries. A miracle is drastic, unbelievable, and earth-shaking. It's the thing that can change your course and put you in a different environment. We've heard of it in *The Greatest Story Ever Told.*

Miracles are not random occurrences; they happen because they are part of a person's predestination. There has to be a situation before there can be a miracle.

Your journey will test you, but make sure to learn from your trials, blessings, and miracles because they will happen.

Prior to achieving the high school world record in the mile relay, I had recruitment letters coming from everywhere, which abruptly ended with the news of my injury. I couldn't pull it together; so I lay in bed, wondering how and why it had happened. After a week of allowing me to feel sorry for myself, my mother said, "Alright, Son, life goes on. This ain't the end of the world." And she was right.

Leadership is a visible thing and since I was the captain of the track team, I still had the responsibility of going to practices and attending every meet to encourage everyone just as a leader should. I didn't envision being able to compete again; so I decided to move on and be happy for the guys. That's all I could do. I didn't run for two months and I walked with a slight limp, and when people looked at me, I could detect sadness in their eyes.

The 4 x 110 and 4 x 220 relay teams had won city without me and qualified for state. Lane Tech was a monster, and I was extremely proud of the guys. With their speed, discipline, drive, and flawless handoffs, nothing less was expected.

When we arrived at the state meet, Coach McCall approached me and said, "Louis, I need to have a conversation with you. The team has decided that we're not gonna participate unless you run."

I said, "Yeah. Okay, right. That's not a funny joke."

He said, "No. We've made that decision."

"What are you talking about? You know I can't run. I'm just barely walking without a limp."

"Something in me believes that you can," Coach insisted.

"Yeah, but we know that's not gonna happen."

"Well, you've got to at least give it a try or we're going home."

"Stop that craziness. Even without me, you have a real good shot at winning this thing."

"Maybe so, but if you don't try, we're going home. The team has voted, and that's where we are," he added firmly.

"Why are you gonna embarrass me like this?"

"Suit up," he continued dismissively. "Come out on the track. It's one hundred degrees today. If it's ever gonna happen, it's gonna happen today!"

"You're gonna embarrass me. All the press is here."

He locked eyes with me and, in an uncompromising tone, said, "Get dressed and warm up."

When I walked onto the track in my uniform, everyone stopped and stared. Since we had a big team, people jumped in and started helping me stretch to get ready. The reporters were visibly astounded.

After warming up, Coach asked, "You ready?"

"Please don't embarrass me like this," I begged one last time.

Still, he insisted. But there was something in Coach McCall's voice when he said, "Trust me. Just trust me," as if he was forcing confidence into me.

I knew my body wasn't ready, but my mind had remained strong. At that moment, I trusted what I believed; great teams are consistent. What makes them great is their consistency of expectation, communication, and execution. We worked hard to have consistency and it came from practice because that was the only way we were going to achieve it.

Although I hadn't run for two months, obediently I positioned myself in the blocks and came out sprinting a time of 21.4.

Exuding extreme confidence, Coach McCall insisted, "This trophy is ours!"

And that was nothing but a miracle!

The meet was highly competitive, and the guys were concerned as to whether or not we could win state.

Following our typical order, I anchored the 4 x 110 and 4 x 220. Over the next two days, we went on to tie East St. Louis for the State Championship. Many of the people who initially recruited me were there, but sadly, I was told, "We've just seen a miracle, but we can't offer you a scholarship on a miracle. We would love to take that chance, but we just can't." I understood.

I went back to my original plan of emulating the people around me and started filling out applications for the Chicago Transit Authority, UPS, and so forth. When August came around, I hadn't received any job offers.

One afternoon, I was at the park when a kid came running up to me and said, "Louis, your mama said to come home right away!" Without a second thought, I sprinted home and rushed through the door to find a man sitting on the sofa, talking to my mother.

He stood up and introduced himself. "Louis, my name is Bob Ehrhart and I'm the coach of Drake University. Do you know a guy by the name of Phil Ferguson?"

"I do."

"Do you know his brother, Ken?"

"Yes. I know his whole family. He went to my high school and we're good friends."

"Well, he came into my office two weeks ago and asked me if I had any track scholarships left. Normally, I don't at this time, everything's committed, but I had one. He said if I did, I should give it to you. I must have been living in a cave because I've never heard of you," he said. "I

41

just left the *Chicago Tribune* and the *Chicago Sun-Times*. I got all these articles," he said pointing at them. And then he shook his head. "I don't know where I've been. I've spoken to all the reporters who've covered you and they said, 'If you're going to take a chance on a guy, take a chance on this guy right here,'" he said, tapping one of the articles.

"Okay," I replied.

"And based on the passion that your friend and these reporters have for you, I'm prepared to offer you a full scholarship for five years."

I was surprised. "Why five?"

"Because we're so committed to our athletes, we give you an extra year just in case you need it."

"What are you talking about? Is this a joke?"

"I'm willing to take a chance. School starts in a week, and I know you'll want to see the university. If you're prepared to at least come look, I have a plane ticket for you."

My mother glanced at me as if she was saying, "I know you're gonna say yeah."

"Okay!" This was another miracle. At that moment, I made the decision I wouldn't need the extra year.

During my years of running track, I attended church with my grandmother. I came to realize that what I was learning had become more than just words. I began living that life with the comprehension that God's love is the greatest mystery of all time.

Two days later, I was on a plane to Iowa, visiting

Drake University. The Drake Stadium was built as a track stadium for the Drake Relays, but they played football there, too. To get to the track, we walked through a tunnel passing underground and entered the stadium through big double doors.

Coach Ehrhart instructed, "Do me a favor. I want you to slowly turn and look above those doors you just came out of." When I turned around, chiseled into the stone, it read, "Through this tunnel pass the greatest athletes in the world". I was done! My decision had just been made. Incidentally, Wilma Rudolph was the first female athlete to participate in the Drake Relays.

Your journey *will* test you, but make sure to learn from your blessings and miracles because they *will* happen.

{4}

VISION

Vision: the act or power of imagination

If you want to be successful, you must comprise a succinct understanding of how to achieve it. Your ability to create a clear, distinct, and specific view of your future is based on your vision. It is absolutely crucial. It's that visual that is always constant. It's the picture you can see in your mind, regardless of whatever else is going on. It's the thing you dream about and the source that keeps your fire burning.

You will not achieve your intended results if you fail to execute on your vision. Just having it isn't enough. Make sure you aren't so focused that you neglect family, friends, and especially, God. *Vision is powerful.*

When people ask how I sustained having a long

career in media, spanning over thirty-four years, the secret is that I never looked backward, down, or side-to-side. I believe it is imperative that you consistently and rapidly look forward because the world and all of its opportunities are based on evolution.

The Internet has nearly taken over our lives. Have you ever imagined magazines becoming obsolete to the *Internet?* Did you think we would progress from cassettes to CDs; and now, streaming music online? Perhaps not, but individuals and companies with vision conceived those evolutionary developments, which is an example of looking forward and keeping up with the changes you encounter on your journey.

Knowledge gives you the basic things
you need for vision.

The world is moving like a bullet train causing transportation, media, fashion, and everything else to become continually revolutionized. You don't have the choice as to whether or not you will keep up with it. It is changing and the aftermath will change you, but to what degree is another conversation. If you plan on being a player, someone who is contributing successfully to this game of life, you must have vision to compete. The more you know, the greater your vision, and then it will become harder to settle. If you don't have any knowledge, the engine has no energy.

My mother was unyielding in teaching me life lessons, and the value of being appreciative is merely one of them. Time and time again, I found both her and my grandmother to be stellar examples. My mother had two jobs, and my grandmother owned the building we lived in. We lived on the first floor, my grandmother occupied the second, and typically another relative lived in the basement. The love my mother and grandmother had for me was undeniable. They provided everything I needed, which constantly left me in a space where I was happy. I had a lot of friends and we had a great deal of fun; so as far as I was concerned, I wasn't deficient in anything. I wasn't aware I had a lack of vision, which meant—I didn't have a lot of need.

One of the things I knew about my mother is that she was insightful and always gave focus to the longer and broader view rather than what was in front of her. She made certain our provisions were met and was persistent in her concern for others. When she prepared a meal, she would make it big enough to share with other families on our block. It was characteristic of her to have me deliver dinner or take pound cake to a neighbor. My mother's vision went further than mine. She instructed me to clean up a neighbor's front yard, despite the fact that the neighbor had children of her own who could have done it. My mother was selfless, and she was teaching me how to be selfless, too. As a part of her vision, she wanted me to care more about the *entire* landscape of things. To bring that image to life, my mother was willing to invest her time and effort.

As far as our lifestyle, naturally, some people had more than us, but I didn't have any concept of how they lived or their means of accommodating their lifestyle; so the comparison wasn't completely made. For some reason, where we lived and what I digested daily wasn't the outcome my mother envisioned for me. She would often drive along Lake Shore Drive just to show me the difference in communities and lifestyles. After taking in the luxury high-rise apartments, to the majestic stone and brick homes lining the streets, she would say, "Son, I want you to be able to get out of our neighborhood and live like this."

I could not reach that vision because I had not embraced the opportunity. When I looked around, it did not take much to notice the overall neighborhood was entirely different from ours. But I came to the conclusion there was something special about the lakefront property. Regardless, I did not think the opportunity to achieve that kind of lifestyle would ever present itself.

"Son, you need to make a decision whether you want to live like this or like we live now. But it's decided by how hard you want to work."

My mother exposed me to the visual side of choices, which taught me that if I worked hard enough, I could create opportunities for myself.

Vision makers are people who see beyond the present. They are like coaches who detect potential in athletes based on raw abilities that the athletes don't yet see in themselves. If you are willing to build on your special talent or gift, and improve the particular set of skills under their guidance, they can take you some place you may not have imagined. And it can happen at any age.

If you do not have vision, you had better hope you run into a vision maker.

These people have a yearning to help you achieve beyond what is normal. They are encouragers, teachers, and mentors who assist you in reaching that place where you can achieve things unimaginable to most. Vision makers have a unique set of skills that allows them to remove you from that comfortable place and guide you through your uncomfortable journey to make sure you arrive. They help you envision yourself in a different space, in a different place. These people are extraordinary and you will become special, too, if you have the opportunity to come in contact with them.

In 1986, I was introduced to Bob Johnson via my best friend, Kevin Newell. Bob wanted Kevin to open a Chicago office for his company, Black Entertainment

Television or BET. Instead, Kevin recommended me for the opportunity. In 1984, the cable industry began investing billions wiring the United States. But at that point, the cable industry was only seven years old. Regardless, I didn't want to work for a startup company after being with Johnson Publishing and Black Enterprise. Although there was something special about Bob, and I really liked him, I wasn't sold. Still, he was persistent, as though he knew something I didn't. He offered me the job a couple of times; however, I declined.

*Allow others to participate in
your vision or dream.*

One evening, he called me and said, "I'm not trying to convince you. I just want you to make the best decision for you." During that time, I loved working for Earl Graves and we had established a great rapport. What I deemed to be impressive was that I didn't have cable television and I'd never heard of BET. But after that conversation, I accepted the job because Bob Johnson sold me on *his vision*. Obviously, since it was Bob Johnson's vision, I didn't have the capacity to see as far as he did. Admittedly, I never thought it was going to become the preeminent black media company of the twenty-first century.

Some people are unwilling to share their success, or what I call *Dirty Little Secrets*, as though they are proprietary, but Bob was extremely generous. His vision was open for people to participate in multiple ways. He gave his inexperienced management team the opportunity to learn essential skills that many of us had not yet experienced anywhere else. To help us achieve a certain degree of success, he believed in sharing both his business and personal relationships. Not only did he allow us to participate in his vision, but he gave us the opportunity to create our own, too.

I am a visionary, but I hire people who build paradigms for success. –Bob Johnson

---

Bob took me to a luncheon with former President Bill Clinton at the National Press Club, which doesn't happen every day. There were about twenty-five people in attendance. Bob exposed people to things we ordinarily would not have been exposed to, such as politicians, diplomats, A-list entertainers, and more. Bob encouraged us to participate on boards and gain knowledge of how they operate. And when it came to preparation, he invested his time in helping me develop. Bob Johnson was *all in, all of the time*.

Being all in, all the time means you are committed to the work and the overall lifestyle. When you get to that point, you will find there are benefits to being all in.

◆ It creates confidence when you know you've done all you can to be successful.

◆ Learning will become continuous, which will increase your knowledge.

◆ It will make your future and journey a lot easier because you will have more control. It helps lessen the highs and lows of success and failure.

◆ It helps with time management, focus, and discipline.

When you think there is nothing else you could have done that is humanly possible, you have peace. *That's all in.*

{5}

DON'T FIGHT BEING SPECIAL

Special: distinguished by some unusual quality;
especially: being in some way superior

Have you ever given someone a compliment only to find that they had a hard time accepting it? When people tell you that you are special, do you believe them? If not, why would you combat a positive statement?

Someone close to you may have identified characteristics or a particular skill set that stands out from the norm. Maybe it was a professional who happened to see or hear you do something that you've accepted as normal, but it isn't. How can others have a perception of you that is vastly different from your own? Sometimes there are reasons that cause a lack of confidence or the ability to view yourself as special.

◆ If you stand out, you are afraid you will not fit in.

◆ You are unwilling to invest in developing that gift.

◆ You are afraid of failure.

◆ You were raised in a dysfunctional or negative environment and your confidence is damaged.

Regardless of the reason, it is time to stop impeding your growth. Whether you are in a professional, athletic, or academic environment, don't fight being special. When other people are able to recognize your skills or talents, and they tell you that you are special, take a closer look. Try to see what they have already found and work on enhancing them.

◆ Start by changing the way you view yourself.

◆ Invest in learning more about your unique qualities or skills.

◆ Find a coach or mentor to help you develop.

Do not buy into the negative label someone else may have given you, or allow a lack of confidence to prevent you from your destiny.

It is good to have a network of friends, but remember, they are your sphere of influence. Don't just let anyone participate in your emotional, spiritual, and mental development. Admit trustworthy, confident, driven, and successful individuals who encourage excellence into your network. Accept guidance from mentors who have conquered their challenges.

For whatever reason, most people believe that a circle of influence only applies to people of a certain age. They think mentoring is for young people. However, mentors are necessary throughout your life. People with a negative thought process can keep you from ever seeing your greatness. Some people have talents that lie dormant because of their inability to believe they exist. Don't let that be you.

Don't fight being special; it is a blessing.

I wear a ring on my right hand that is of particular significance to me. My grandmother gave it to me when I was a baby. Losing her only son was so devastating that when my mother became pregnant with me, my grandmother prayed for her to have a son. And when she did, my grandmother believed I was God's gift to help her deal with the loss. Although I was just a baby, she believed I was special and placed a diamond ring on my finger as a reminder.

Each year, they had the setting expanded so it would fit my finger as I grew. By the time I was seven, the ring had been expanded so many times that the diamond became loose, and I lost it. We looked everywhere for the diamond but could not find it. A year later, on the middle of the living room floor that had been vacuumed countless times, they found the diamond. At that point, my grandmother decided to keep the diamond until I graduated from high school. When I did, she gave it to me as a gift, in the setting I have now.

Over the years, both my mother and grandmother were persistent in their claims that I was special. But I fought believing it because I didn't like the feeling of being different. I couldn't see anything in myself that was any different from anyone else so I kept pushing back.

In time, it seemed that through their faith and belief in me, they spoke it into existence. I began to believe I was good when it came to track. Then I worked harder to become better than average. To this day, I work at being great in my professional career. If you do not believe that you are special, how can you develop in a particular area?

◆ Other people can help identify your special gift or talent, but it is up to you to activate it.

◆ There are enough joy killers waiting to do damage and they need a negative, doubting mindset to be successful. Do not give them yours.

◆ Believe that ordinary people can achieve extraordinary things.

Discovering your talents is a part of your journey, which may be revealed at different stages of your life. Do not fight being special; it is a blessing.

{6}

HARD WORK

Hard: physically or mentally difficult: not easy

When I was young, I worked hard at everything I did because I did not believe there was any other way to do it. Today, there are people who do not know the definition of hard work because that definition has changed over time. Rather than criticize our children and young adults, it is our responsibility to teach them to be the best they can be. That will happen when they are able to be challenged and uncomfortable because it is only to their benefit. It needs to occur as early as possible since we know life is difficult.

Some people identify hard work with how much time they put in. They do not have any concept beyond that. When it comes to your career, this world is more competitive than you may realize. You never know how many people you are competing against for a position because the applicants are coming in from around the globe. To win, you have to be at the top of your game. Opportunities are hard to come by, so when you are given one, make the most out of it by doing your best and working hard.

I want people to excel and, sometimes, they need nothing more than the opportunity. However, inside of that opportunity, they need to learn what hard work is all about, which in return will teach them about their commitment, passion, and drive.

---

*It really takes specialized skills
to get the job done right.*

Against everyone's advice, I hired a young man right out of college. I gave him a job that was bigger than his experience and knowledge, knowing it would challenge him. Then, I told his boss to make it work. I wanted him to understand what it took to fill that position. The responsibility that came with it was more than what he was willing to invest, and he struggled. One day, his boss came into my office and told me we had broken him. The young man was going to quit. I said, "When he comes in, tell him I want to see him."

An hour later, he entered my office. After studying his demeanor, I said, "Let's go for a walk." I took him outside and gave him the only option available. "You are not quitting, you owe me. You will not embarrass me like this. They told me not to hire you and I went out on a limb against everybody. So, you are not leaving until I ask you to leave. Let's go back inside so we can get some more work done."

The reason I didn't let him leave was that he didn't know what hard work was, and I wasn't done with his lesson. Over time, he grew into that position and learned to do it well. Years later, every time he runs into me, he smiles. That young man has had incredible success.

In an effort to prepare people to be successful anywhere they go, we have to teach them.

- Make sure the preparation is consistent with the challenge.

- Do not run away from the goal. Meet it head on.

- Envision yourself doing the work.

- Use your mental and emotional aggression to push through challenges.

- Make sure you understand the job and the goal is bigger than yourself. Your success or lack of it can open or close a door for someone else.

———◆———

*Some people do not know what hard work
is. They think it is about time spent. It is not
about the time, it is about the intensity.*

———◆———

When it came to business, Earl Graves was tough. He had a military sergeant management style and was no-nonsense. He was the type of manager that when I saw him or spoke to him, I had to be prepared because he would always ask me a question about the business in a very serious manner. Mr. Graves was the guy who looked through your files. He wanted to see the most up-to-date letters, proposals, and information on each client and their industry. He took preparation to another level and I learned to do the same.

Late one evening, Mr. Graves flew into town. My boss and I picked him up from the airport and took him to the office. It was the end of the day, but Mr. Graves wanted the entire team to *role-play*. He was the client and we were the salesmen. That night, Mr. Graves kept us in the office until around eleven-thirty. After role-playing, he looked at the whole team and said, "You're all terrible. I don't see how you'll sell your way out of a paper bag. Come back in the morning at seven o'clock. There will be a note on the door letting you know if you have your jobs."

I was so upset when I was leaving the parking lot, I went through the exit lane and scraped my car door against the pay machine because I was too close. I didn't sleep well that night. When I showed up at seven o'clock the next morning, I found that I still had my job. That situation taught me a lesson in 360° preparation. Whether it is internal or external, do not take preparation for granted. You have to do the work because it is not going to happen automatically. When you believe in the value your product and consumers bring, be willing to fight for it.

People say they don't have time,
but some of that free time isn't free.

{7}

THAT UNCOMFORTABLE PLACE

Uncomfortable: feeling discomfort or uneasiness

At the recommendation of John H. Johnson, I moved out of my mother's house and relocated to downtown Chicago in close proximity to Johnson Publishing. Surprisingly, I was accommodating the vision my mother had for me years earlier. I loved living downtown; and of course, I wanted my mother to move, too. Ultimately, she agreed.

Do not be afraid to operate in an uncomfortable space; it is only going to help you grow.

Even though my mother was moving into her own spacious and beautiful place with a direct view of the lake, it was difficult for her. I noticed as she was packing up her belongings, she was crying. She was leaving the home she had occupied for nearly forty years on the West Side of Chicago. My mother encouraged me to pursue my journey, which took me away from what I was used to. Watching my mother made me realize the move was now taking her out of her comfort zone as well. It was where her memories were, her friends lived, and everything she was connected to resided. My mother was transitioning— to a new place, *an uncomfortable place.*

It is not uncommon to have difficulty in a place of unfamiliarity, where you will feel out of your comfort zone for a period of time. The key is to understand you will determine the duration. It happens when you move from one place to another and when you change jobs, careers, or even positions. You have seen it occur with athletes when they are traded to another team. The same way they have to make necessary adjustments to fit comfortably in their new environment, you will too. Until that happens, you will be in an uncomfortable place. Some people adapt quicker and without incident in comparison to others. Why? It's a result of preparation, experience, or confidence. When it comes to change, a little uncertainty will always follow.

One afternoon, I was walking over to my mailbox when a dog came racing toward me with two people chasing after him. He darted past me, slipped into my garage, and lay down beneath one of my cars. Apologetic for the inconvenience, the owners of the dog went into my garage to retrieve him. Regardless of how hard they tried, they could not get their dog to *willingly* come out. Finally, I knelt down and looked at the dog. He appeared to be completely content and had no intention of moving. But after talking to him, and some prodding, he came out.

When you commit to making a transition to something new, take time to prepare appropriately. Never underestimate the difficulty of change.

What I began to notice was nearly every time they opened their door, the dog seemed to run. He was not familiar with their house and he was clearly in an uncomfortable place as they had recently moved in.

When you commit to making a transition to something new, these things will help:

- ◆ Take time to prepare appropriately.
- ◆ Become familiar with the environment, the change in your routine, and the people.

◆ Do not underestimate the difficulty of change.

◆ Give yourself a timeline to learn your environment and find things that will make you comfortable.

When it comes to making a career move, people have the tendency to evaluate the individual who occupied the position prior to them. Often, they make an inaccurate assumption regarding what the job involves. If someone makes a job look easy, it may be *for that individual*, but it does not mean it will be for you. Find mentorship or counsel from someone who has already done it. This will bring more accuracy to your assessment of the position. Then, use your vision and see yourself doing the job before you find yourself in an uncomfortable place.

Being in an uncomfortable place is the way to set goals, have vision, and stretch yourself beyond what you have ever done or think you can do.

When I attended Drake University, I realized the move from high school to college was one of the most difficult transitions that will put you in an uncomfortable place. The bar is raised from day one. As you know, once you enter college, you have crossed an invisible threshold where *you* are accountable for your actions. From that point on, your teachers and parents are exempt. You cannot blame your professors because no one is going to listen and no one is going to care. Whether or not you go to class, pass, or fail, the accountability shifts totally to you. No one is going to tell you when to get up, go to bed, wash your clothes, or eat because—it is your responsibility. College is one of the major transitions in life. It takes preparation and maturity to help you adapt.

You may think it is easier to avoid being uncomfortable. To the contrary, that is exactly what you *should* want. Being in an uncomfortable place is the way to set goals, have vision, and stretch yourself beyond what you have ever done or think you can do. It will help you succeed in business and life.

{8}

MATURITY IS A JOURNEY OF ITS OWN

Maturity: the condition of being fully developed

There is something remarkable that can help you in your career and personal life that you cannot envision until you actually acquire it. It is clearly discernible when you do and even more detectable when you have not. This attitude and persona allows you to be more in control than you were previously. It is a peaceful, calming effect or surety that enables you to make better decisions in different circumstances. That something is maturity.

At some point, you will become mindful of the things you have done throughout your journey. More precisely, you will be aware of the results and consequences created by your decisions. Therefore, you have the propensity to distinguish whether or not you have matured. The moment you find yourself in a situation and can acknowledge that in the past you would have made a different type of decision, it is evidence that you are growing. When you look through the rearview mirror, that emotional growth comes from understanding and realizing the impact you have had on your life, as well as the lives of others. When you have matured, it is displayed in your behavior.

There are social, spiritual, emotional, business, and financial maturity. It is demonstrated in your behavior, encompassing a broader scope than what most people would consider.

◆ Social maturity involves the proper way to relate to people at different stages as well as how to respect authority.

◆ Spiritual maturity is an ongoing process that encompasses your journey of faith.

◆ Emotional maturity speaks to how you are able to engage, communicate, and make decisions in situations that are extremely uncomfortable.

◆ Business maturity enables you to be more strategic, tactical, and gives clarity to the big picture.

◆ Financial maturity allows you to make better decisions in regard to your spending, savings, and investing.

When you regularly work toward improving your maturity, you will gain more control over your emotions and reactions. Why? You will be more confident of the outcome. Your emotional and high-strung nature tends to dissipate as you grow into a more flexible and confident individual. What you will gain is a greater sense of peace and assurance in your abilities and the outcome. In time, you will realize that you are predisposed to acting with wisdom and more inclined to help people along the way. Maturity will give you the rearview mirror reference that you didn't notice before.

Ego should not be the thing that holds us back from the greatness God has set us here for.

Although many have yet to reach maturity, some of them will be great once they do. At times, I encounter people who do not understand what it is I am trying to teach them because they are not mature enough. My goal is to plant the seed of maturity in people so they start to have a greater reflection on their behaviors and circumstances in life. The process will help you begin to see yourself with an honest deliberation regarding your actions. Whether or not they are good or bad, you will learn the value of taking your actions under greater consideration.

Maturity means having personal jurisdiction, a spirit

of humility, authentic gratitude, and an honest character. Additionally, a willingness to learn and gain more knowledge, combined with experience, is a part of the process.

I meet a lot of people who are highly intelligent, yet immature. It hinders their ability to make the right decision. If you want to reach a mature level, the way to accomplish that is through *reflection* and *evaluation*. Reflect on and evaluate your behavior, circumstances, achievements, and pitfalls. It is an important part of the process. I do not believe you can mature without reflection and evaluation. At times, it is easy and there are other moments when it is more difficult.

Early in my career, I began doing a personal reflection. I would go on sales calls and give my presentation but as soon as I left the building, I would begin to reflect. Was that a good presentation? Was I bad? What could I have done differently? All kinds of thoughts regarding my attitude, behavior, preparedness, and everything else received an evaluation, and it wasn't always good. The key is, if you are going to do an evaluation, make it an honest assessment of your behavior and the consequences. While people may give one assessment, my personal evaluation and reflection may be different regardless of what I am told. That is my way of staying balanced.

A personality trait that can hurt your maturity is when ego comes into play. Ego is when you are in that space where there is no self-awareness. It is the place that makes you take uncalculated risks and doesn't allow you to listen to anyone. I can understand if you are the Heavyweight Champion of the World, Super Bowl Champions, an Olympic Gold Medalist or simply number one. But there are only a few at that level and the metrics are extremely apparent when you are number one.

———◆———

You can take risks. Just make sure
they are calculated risks.

———◆———

For most of us, there is room to learn, develop, and get better. Regardless of what people tell us or how great we feel about ourselves, there is still a way to get there. Even the greatest of orators may mispronounce a word or stumble, but they learn from it and keep going. Ego should not be the thing that holds us back from the greatness God has set us here for.

It is difficult to witness a lack of maturity, particularly in business, because that deficiency is holding back progress. When it comes to teaching, mentoring, advising, or even handling an immature individual, it is tough. The question becomes: What do you do? Instead of ignoring it, make an effort to reveal it to the individual so they can voluntarily make a change. It is important to try to show someone that they can be so much better if they would do some things differently. Give them insight into how making better decisions, being more in control, and placing themselves in thought-provoking environments will help them grow. The only things a lack of maturity can do are smother your achievements and impede your progress.

If you want to help someone who is immature, identify the cause. It may be a lack of experience, vision, or knowledge, but there are times when it is a combination or all of them.

Some people have never been in an uncomfortable place, whether that entails hard work or being challenged with difficult situations. If you haven't pushed through that wall to get to the other side, it is your lack of accepting the challenge that will hurt your maturity. But there is always something you will need to overcome in order to have some type of emotional development. Some people are born with physical challenges they have to overcome, and they may mature faster than others because of them. People who grew up without their parents are sometimes forced to mature faster because they may assume a role that no one else is there to fill. There are many reasons for one's maturity to develop early. If you have siblings, friends, or peers who are mature for their age, you will find there is a story behind it.

A lack of maturity is not a matter of gender versus gender or rich versus poor. There are parents who are well off who do not give their children everything because they want them to take the initiative to do things on their own. Coaches do the same thing; they put athletes in particular positions that are difficult for the purpose of growth. There were times when I had to practice with the cross-country team and I did the same workouts they did to expand my endurance and get stronger. Of course, I didn't want to do it, but my coach put me in that situation. There will be opportunities that will place us in a position to help others mature, and it is our responsibility to help guide them through the process. Do not walk away from opportunities to pass on what you have been blessed to learn.

Some people can display an out-of-control ego but when their head hits the pillow at night, they know the real deal.

When I was in my mid-twenties, I was a young executive at Johnson Publishing. I was a hot head with an uncontrollable temper and thought I knew much more than I actually did. Having been a decent athlete, I did not think there was much more to learn. Based on my view, I was in a comfortable place and already thought I was successful. However, I really hadn't achieved an ounce of success in regard to business. I certainly didn't have sufficient self-awareness or understand how people viewed me. And at that point, I didn't care. As far as I was concerned, neither bosses nor peers could teach me anything. But time had no problem providing evidence that I was wrong.

One day, John H. Johnson pulled me into his office concerning a situation where I had inappropriately communicated. Although I was given the opportunity to acknowledge and correct the situation, I didn't. Since my maturity wasn't completely intact, I could not allow myself to view my behavior as disrespectful or wrong; so I was fired.

In retrospect, my firing from Johnson Publishing may have been a necessary part of my journey. I was not fired for performance. The reason I was fired was due to obnoxious, disrespectful communication—in other words, a lack of maturity. What I am saying is: eventually the consequences *will* catch up with you.

The growth process to reach maturity requires a constant and honest evaluation of your behavior. Maturity will not happen without it. I believe some people can display an out-of-control ego, but when their head hits the pillow at night, they know the real deal.

When you demonstrate a lack of maturity, people are not going to line up and tell you. Instead, they may cut you off or refrain from inviting you into their space. If you want to know what you really look and sound like, surround yourself with a core group of people who will be bluntly honest and who you trust will tell you the truth.

That is the greatest lesson that has helped me progress from a decent executive to a better executive.

There are many occasions when I talk with people I trust and say, "Let me tell you what I did," which is sort of my way of checking in. Then I ask them what they think I need to do. Do not let your pride keep you from asking for constructive criticism or advice. Admitting that you need to learn something, improve in some way, or that you did something wrong is a process. When you do, it contributes to your growth and helps the situation. Someone who is still in the growth process will apologize for his or her behavior without justification. Be willing to recognize that you need work and then be prepared to do it. Sometimes situations will try to pull you away from your personal growth and that means there will be occasions when you have to turn—and just walk away.

It may seem fun to speak your mind and do whatever you please, but it has consequences. The benefits of maturity are that you are able to manage not only yourself but also your environment. You may have heard someone say, "He's very mature for his age." It is an indication that maturity stands out in any environment and makes you a leader at any age. Whether it is through knowledge or decision-making, people take notice.

When it comes to making a hiring decision that can help identify a person's maturity, ask specific questions. One of the questions I ask is, "Can you tell me something that you've overcome?" A mature person will answer it on the dime. They don't have to think about it because they know what it is. It is something that changed them in some form or another. Mature people are inclined to be confident in their growth and in their communication of what made them grow. As you listen, you will hear confidence in their storytelling. When I interview candidates, I ask them about challenges. If they can't answer the question, that means they have not evaluated some of the things throughout their journey that they could have done better.

{9}

UNDERSTAND YOUR ROLE

---

*Role: the part that someone has in a family,
society, or other group*

When the black car pulled up to the curb, the driver
jumped out and greeted me while opening my door.
Lightly tossing my briefcase on the backseat, I sat inside
and leaned back, taking a deep breath. It was the end of
a long week, but I had yet another commitment to keep.
Traveling frequently made the driver a familiar face. He
was one of the guys who typically drove me to the airport
or picked me up upon my return.

"Where are you going today?" he asked.

"Skiing," I replied.

"What? You don't seem like a skier."

"I'm not, and I don't like it. But I lost a bet to a friend."

He paused as though he were deliberating. Then he asked, "Can I step out of my role and have a conversation with you?"

"Sure."

"You know, as a driver, we're not supposed to listen to anyone's conversation. But of course, you know we do. We just don't talk about it."

Laughing at his admission, I said, "Yeah," offering a slight nod.

"Over the years, as I've been driving you, I've listened to your conversations and you always seem to be a little stressed."

"Okay," I conceded, waiting for his point.

"It's because you haven't accepted your role."

I sat up a little more, realizing he was trying to have a deeper conversation with me.

"So, what is my role?"

"Louis, some people are born to serve, not to be served. And *you* were born to serve."

"I don't want to hear that—because I want to have some fun, too," I joked.

"No, you'll have fun when you accept that as your role. And you'll get joy out of giving other people joy," he added, with a serene expression reflected in the rearview mirror.

There was an undeniable truth to what he shared with me that day. And although it took a little time to acknowledge, I have accepted that my role is to serve people with the understanding I am paying toward a bigger cause.

I believe it is important that I inform and educate people in my purview. Whether they work for me, are part of my foundation, or people I know, I am sharing what I have learned. Some of the information is by way of experience, while the balance is a result of the best combination of ingredients that have been poured into me.

God has positioned people in my life to serve as mentors or to guide me along parts of my journey, just as God has done for you. At the end of the day, we will find ourselves in situations we know we don't deserve. Therefore, it is our responsibility to give others an opportunity to excel and progress even further than we have.

Picture yourself making your way down a bustling street distracted by a conversation you are having over the phone. By a narrow margin, you missed stepping into a pothole while crossing to the other side. The next day, you are crossing that same crowded street with a few colleagues and notice that a piece of paper is concealing the pothole. With your colleagues headed straight for it, do you let one of them step in it and perhaps break an ankle? Would you warn them or is your preference to 'let them learn the same way I did'?

I have wondered where I would be now if more

people had shared their knowledge and taught me lessons through positive affirmations so I could avoid making unapprised decisions when I was a young adult.

Once you reach the point where you dislike the rules that are established, become a game changer and you can make different decisions.

In 1984, I interviewed for a position as an Account Executive with Johnson Publishing. I showed up prepared and polished, right down to my red shoes. After a great interview, John H. Johnson offered me the position, but warned, "Never come in here with those red shoes on again. And fix the button on your shirt."

I didn't know the button on my shirt was broken nor was I aware that my top-of-the-line, red Fotie's were not appropriate. Then, he concluded by suggesting that I move downtown into a building he recommended.

When you are advised of something you are not prepared to hear, the initial effect can be stinging because naturally, it doesn't feel good. The embarrassment causes you to question whether or not others have shared the same sentiment but chose not to inform you. For a moment, you may feel a little uncomfortable. When emotions enter the equation, the decision to act on what was said, fight it, or think about it can cause discord. Perhaps you will dismiss their opinion, maintain your position and resign to being right, as you label that individual *wrong*. Although you could not convince me that I wasn't sharply dressed, I thought about it and immediately understood his point.

Basically, John H. Johnson had told me, 'You are all wrong and you need to be fixed.' Nevertheless, he gave me the job after just one interview, along with a solution to each issue he cited. Mr. Johnson had a concise vision as to the type of executives he wanted under his leadership. At the time, my shoes weren't acceptable to him, but he was my boss and it was *his* company. Once you reach the point when you dislike the rules that are established, become a game changer and you can make decisions. Michael Jordan didn't ride the bus to his home games; he drove behind them in his jet-black 512 TR Ferrari. Kobe Bryant went to practice in a helicopter, and it was acceptable because they were game changers. One of the dirty little secrets I came to understand is that people make exceptions for game changers and I hadn't proven myself *yet*. Anyone who makes a difference in any environment is someone who people will treat differently.

People expect more from game changers and if that comes with an ego, just live up to it and be consistent. Consistency is used when describing top athletes. If a basketball player is known as a high scorer, he is expected to maintain a high-scoring average. The owners, management, and fans want to know you will consistently deliver for them. They don't want thirty points one night and twelve another. And people will expect you to make everyone around you better, whether you have a leadership title or not.

Receiving the baton from Dennis Kern at the city qualifying meet.

The final of the 4 x 220 at the 1974 State Championship.

The Fearsome Foursome with the State Championship trophy in 1974.

THE NATIONAL FEDERATION OF
STATE HIGH SCHOOL ATHLETIC ASSOCIATIONS

TRACK OR FIELD AWARD

presented to

TIMOTHY KLEIN, LOUIS CARR, KEVIN NEWELL, DENNIS KERN

Lane Technical High School, Chicago, Illinois

in recognition for establishing

NATIONAL INTERSCHOLASTIC RECORD

MILE RELAY (Indoor)

event

3 Minutes, 19.5 Seconds

record achieved

62nd Chicago Public League Indoor Meet
CHICAGO, ILLINOIS
name and location of meet

MARCH 29, 1974
date

JUNE 11, 1974
Date Presented

National Federation Executive Secretary

National Federation Track Committee Chairman

LANE TECH
TRACK & FIELD
AWARDS BANQUET

NATIONAL RECORD HOLDERS

LANES MILE RELAY TEAM - TIME 3:19.5

Kevin Newell, Dennis Kern, Timothy Klein, Louis Carr

Honoring:
The 1974 Track Team
STATE CHAMPIONS

Friday, June 7, 1974 - - 7:30 p.m.
Johnny Weigelt's
3900 N. Damen Ave. Chicago, Illinois

Lane Tech Track & Field Awards Banquet program.

Close-up: Louis Carr

by Jody Mihalec

Louis Carr is captain of Lane's Track Team, runs the 50 yard dash in 5.4; 60 in 6.4; 100 in 9.9; 220 in 21.2 and the 440 in 49.1. It's hard to believe that three years ago, equipped with so much speed Louis never considered competing on Lane's Track Team. It wasn't until a broken arm seperated him from football in his sophomore year, that track even entered his mind. Track now plays such an important role, it's almost his life.

Even during the summer months Louis is hard at work at what he does best, running. Last summer he joined the Chicago Zephyrs track club, competed in the college division against such schools as SIU and University of Illinois and was victorious in the 440 relays at the Lakefront Festival Meet. He is hoping this summer he will make the Junior National Olympic team that meets in Europe.

Louis believes he has the answer when it comes to the succeessfulness of the Track Team. "I think that the Track Team is successful because we have to do everything ourselves; the school isn't giving us anything. The most successful teams I believe, are the teams that have to do the most work on their own. Another reason is that we have a good radical balance. If you look throughout the state, we're the most well balanced. The coaches and the team members work well together. The coaches make the decisions and we do the running. Coaches McCall and Lewis deserve a lot of credit; they took the Track Team when Lane had ideas of eliminating track. They went

You've heard of the "Fearsome Foursome" in football. Well, Lane's Track Team has a "Fearsome Foursome" of their own. They are l-r: Kevin Newell, the best sprinter in the city; Dennis Kern, the best half-miler in the city; Tim Klein, the best hurdler in the city; and Louis Carr, the best anchor man in the city. Together they make up the best mile-relay team in the nation. Their time of 3:19.5 set a national record.

from a 5 man team of no bodies, to a state caliber team in 6 years."

"Are we capable of taking the State title? "DEFINITELY! We've come so close in the post years, but didn't take it. The coaches always thought we could, but the team never did. Now we believe we can do it. Before we'd go to a meet and fear names like Howard Jones, Mike McFarland, Max Tolen and we used to feel that we had to run against them, now we feel they have to run against us."

From the above statements, I'd venture to describe Louis as outgoing. So, says Louis, would most of his friends. He however feels differently, viewing himself as a quiet person, someone who likes to daydream and think alot.

His favorites include; Sandford and Son, red, the Godfather, chicken and dressing, Stylistics, Steve Williams and Lee Evans.

Beside taking city and state and making Junior National Olympic Team, another goal he is striving to achieve is to win the 220 in the state meet in less than 21 seconds flat. Louis Carr will achieve most if not all his goals. I guess I feel that way because I've seen him run in races, and on that track with Louis there were lots of people headed in the same direction......but he always got there first.

Lane Tech 1974 Track and Field Outdoor Schedule

4-20	Niles N. Viking Invitational	V/FS	1:00 p.m.
*4-27	Proviso W. Invitational	V/FS	1:00 p.m.
4-30	City College Relay Finals	Var.	12:30 p.m.
*5-4	Thornton Invitational	Var.	3:15 p.m.
5-7	City Track Prelims-Winnemac Pk.	Var.	3:15 p.m.
5-8	City Field Prelims-Winnemac Pk.	FS	3:15 p.m.
5-8	City Track Prelims-Winnemac Pk.	FS	3:15 p.m.
5-10	City Field Prelims-Winnemac Pk.	Var.	3:15 p.m.
5-17	Outdoor City Finals-U. of Chicago-Stagg		3:15 p.m.
5-24,25	State Trials-U. of Chicago-Stagg		3:15 p.m.
5-24,25	STATE FINALS-Eastern III.-Charleston, III.		

* chartered bus

Article in 1974 from Lane Tech newspaper.

My mother and I after my college graduation.

Me, my grandmother, and Mike Morgan.

My wife, Diane, and I at our wedding on May 17, 1986.

My mother, me, and Dad at my wedding.

Mike Morgan, Kevin Newell, and me.

Me and former Governor of Alabama, George Wallace.

Me and Bob Johnson at a BET sales conference.

My wife, Diane, and I at a fundraiser in our home for Mayor Richard Daley.

Hanging with Clint Culpepper, President of Sony Screen Gems.

Ray Goulbourne, Cedric The Entertainer, and I at the BET Honors.

Me and automobile magnate Bill Shack with his wife.

Me with the Chairman and CEO of BET, Debra Lee.

Tony Cornelius and I at ABFF Awards pre-reception.

Former Vice President Al Gore and me at Bob Johnson's home.

Me, Russell Simmons, and former President Clinton at The National Press Club.

President Obama and I at a neighborhood fundraiser.

{ 10 }

REINVENT YOURSELF

Reinvent: to present (something) in a different or new way

Throughout your life, it is expected that you will pass through many environments and meet countless individuals. Since it is a part of your journey, be open to evolution and learn different or new ways to accomplish things. Keep an open mind and possess a willingness to engage or interact in diverse environments.

Take a minute to observe your environment and note some of the things that have evolved from what they used to be. Now, imagine how rapidly the rest of the world is changing. That means you have to be willing to change so you don't end up stuck in time. I have always wanted to be a person who was current and I have done it with my management style, various media platforms, technology, communication, fashion, and other areas; *it's my business.* If you want to be on top of your business, there are a few ways for you to stay current.

◆ Become familiar with what is in and what is not.

◆ Reinvent yourself based on how fast the world is changing.

◆ Do not be the person who has to be made over.

◆ Remember that it takes more energy to catch up than to keep up.

◆ Be open to doing things differently.

◆ Surround yourself with a diverse group of people.

Reading allows you to gain knowledge of the reasons industries evolve and reinvent themselves. Learn where things are heading so you can be current, too.

———————◆———————

To reinvent yourself, you have to expand your boundaries of information and communication.

———————◆———————

Several years ago, I was a member of a club in Chicago. Over dinner, I was having a conversation with a member who stated she was leaving the organization. She said, "I've done everything that needed to be done." It seemed as though her remark caused everyone at the table to have a look of confusion. She didn't say she had been fired, she was tired, or that she was going somewhere to do something different. She had not done everything that needed to be done; she did everything that she could do. The problem was that she did not know how to reinvent herself so she could take the organization to the next level. That may have been due to a lack of vision, will, passion, skill, or something else. The bottom line is, there had not been a reinvention.

If you find yourself in the same place, without advancing and nothing is changing, you probably haven't reinvented yourself or your vision. I often hear people say, "I'm doing the best I can do." Most of the time, I believe them, but therein lies the problem. If their best is not good enough to move the organization forward or to a different place, their best is *just not good enough*.

People who lead teams and companies have to constantly think about reinventing themselves in preparation for the next phase of their business. It is important to understand what the next transition of that industry is going to be and the role the company or team will play.

- ◆ Clearly define how you are going to accomplish that transition.

- ◆ Determine how you are going to help your team evolve.

- ◆ Be open to having your organization engage with people who may think differently than you do.

I have seen organizations that do not grow. They can be small nonprofit organizations or big conglomerates— and their growth stops. Why? They don't want to engage or socialize with anyone outside of their circle. Most of the time, they have no interest in observing how other people are doing things. As a result, they tend to brush off the success of others as something that's going to come and go versus learning from it. There are ways to reinvent yourself to be more progressive in business.

- Expand the boundaries of information and communication.

- Step out and engage in things that are out of the norm for you. It may happen through physical engagement, reading, or just listening.

- Work to acquire some understanding of what people are doing differently and how it is working for them.

I have an inherent desire to learn and acquire an in-depth knowledge of things, especially when it supports my ability to be an effective leader. If someone who works for me asks for advice, I should be able to accommodate. That doesn't mean I need to be the subject-matter expert, but it is necessary for me to have some type of feel and understanding of my business so I can offer direction.

There came a point when I had to reinvent a new version of the way I led people because I only knew one way. That was to push them and work them into the ground.

Over the course of time, I had to learn how to continue to drive them while offering something more. I had to give them things that would be priceless, and that was knowledge.

Being able to reinvent yourself is the key for anyone who wants to grow.

The first step was for me to realize they could learn from someone other than me. You may think a consultant cannot advise you on something they do not do every day, but they can. How do you get through to someone you only talk with once every two weeks? Furthermore, how can someone get through to you? I found that, at times, outside consultants could teach my team better than I could. Remove your pride and focus on the results. Change is good.

My second step was to realize I could learn something from someone who was not in my business. Initially, I thought I could only learn or be taught by a subject-matter expert. Nevertheless, it did not take long before I discovered that philosophy was incorrect. For growth purposes, I took the steps to reinvent myself and accept other ways of being taught. What would I lose if I just tried it? Nothing. What I had was a tremendous opportunity for an upside. When you are winning with an old set of rules, adjust to the new set and win with those, too. If you keep doing the same things that you are familiar with or comfortable doing, the results will not change. Try something new; reinvent yourself.

{11}

YOUR IMAGE SPEAKS

Image: a mental conception held in common by members of a group and symbolic of a basic attitude and orientation

When people see you for the first time, it only takes seconds for them to develop an opinion. In the corporate arena, your image, along with your knowledge and behavior, can be a representation of your professional competency.

In your personal life, your image matters just the same because you never know who you may run into and where that may be. My grandmother was a former hairdresser, and her image was important to her. She always matched her shoes and purse, wore long gloves, and kept her hair nicely done. She was treated with respect wherever she went.

Respect must be earned before it is given, which is

why your image is so important. If you are trying to fit into a specific business culture, there is an easy way to begin. Make yourself familiar with the company culture and then create your personal brand. Keep in mind, if you are in a position that will cause you to interact with people outside of your office, consider the culture and the presence they have established, and fit in. For example, when I have a business meeting, normally, I wear a suit with a shirt and tie. However, when I call on the entertainment industry, my attire is business casual.

That first impression may be the only one you get to make. If you are not at your best, it could cost you valuable opportunities. Given that your image is a personal persona that you develop, take it under careful consideration. When it comes to image, I have my own dirty little secrets.

- ◆ Preparing the night before allows you to reflect on the type of image you want to create.

- ◆ The persona you want to portray has to be consistent with your vision.

- ◆ Your business attire may vary depending on the goal or objective.

- ◆ Consider the people you are trying to influence or impress.

- ◆ Ensure that your mental and physical preparedness are aligned.

You should care about your image
because it always extends beyond you.

The reason image is significant to me is because I clearly understand it is much bigger than me. I am a representation of my family, company, industry, and many organizations; as well as the people in them. The way you show up determines how people relate to you—there is more to your image than the way you dress.

- ◆ Good grooming is essential to your image. People may not tell you, but they will talk about you.

- ◆ Your written and verbal communication is reflective of your competency and attention to details. That is one of the reasons a corporation will employ those with excellent communication skills.

- ◆ Social media has become a primary way to identify your true character and habits. Pay attention to the information you share online.

- ◆ Whether or not you are aware of your body language, it speaks volumes and displays your emotional intent. Your facial expressions can speak before you do.

*When you think of your image, understand
that it is not just physical; it is mental,
emotional, and about your preparedness.*

There was a young man who came in for an interview by way of a recommendation. He was a recent college graduate and standout athlete. When I asked him what he knew about our company, he replied, "I just want to see how much you're offering before I start preparing myself."

I decided he needed to learn a lesson so that it would help him in the future. I went ahead and had him interviewed so he could understand how ill-prepared he was.

Afterward, I said, "Okay, nice meeting you."

He asked what the next step was, and I stated, "There isn't one. You were unprepared."

Regardless of where you are, someone is always observing you. When you think of your image, understand that it is not just physical; it is mental, emotional, and about your preparedness.

- ◆ Present yourself in a polished and confident manner so you are perceived as a professional.

- ◆ Demonstrate that you want to fit in with the corporate culture.

- Always be stylish. Study the trends and stay current.

- Make sure your clothes fit properly.

- Do not over accessorize.

- Be professional when selecting a hairstyle.

- Have good shoes.

- Your image and your company's image should be congruent.

{ 12 }

INSERT YOURSELF

Insert: to cause (someone) to be involved in an activity

*As you know, when it comes to your image, confi-*dence matters. There will be more than a few occasions when you will have to rely on your confidence as a way to insert yourself into networking opportunities. Remember that confidence comes from knowledge, hard work, understanding, and overcoming challenges. Your confident image can help open doors that otherwise may be locked, especially when people are not familiar with you. However, there is more to networking than just showing up at an event. It presents the opportunity for you to build relationships based on trust and determines how you can create mutually beneficial situations. When it comes to your overall success in business, building a solid network of strong relationships is not only necessary, it's valuable. It may be the only way to reach a decision-maker and it can be an effective method of creating business opportunities.

Networking in professional settings is an approach to not only introduce yourself but also your company, services, and products to potential clients. Initially, learning to network teaches you how to operate in an uncomfortable space. If you are in sales, being able to insert yourself should be first nature. For some, learning how to insert yourself into a conversation can be challenging. But if you don't try, can you imagine the lost opportunities?

Have you ever received an invitation to a social gathering and declined because you didn't know anyone who would be attending? What happens when you are at a meeting and you notice everyone conversing in intimate groups but you aren't in one of them? Improving social skills takes work, but it is wiser than walking away or not participating. Although you may not be *invited* to join a conversation, all it takes is skill and confidence to do it on your own.

Taking the initiative to interact socially will help you gain a better understanding of people and it will develop your social skills. In the Louis Carr Internship Foundation, we teach our students to meet as many people as they can, introduce themselves, and ask for advice. John H. Johnson said, "Don't wait for someone to introduce you. You have to let people know you're in the room."

Depending on your environment, some people may ignore you because they are unfamiliar with you. Yet, they are there to network, just as you are. How do you overcome that situation? Make yourself known by inserting yourself into the conversation or by starting one—the success of your business may rely on it.

Depending on your environment, some people may ignore you because they are unfamiliar with you. Insert yourself.

Years ago, I attended industry-specific conventions. Given that I had the same professional objective as the people at the conventions, it was my responsibility to make the environment work. To accomplish that goal, I had to insert myself into the discussions taking place. If I didn't, I may have missed out on valuable opportunities. That was easy because I wasn't there to make friends; I was there to network and sometimes that took creativity. I'd tell my colleague, "Let's stand by the elevator." Why? Because when people left the convention, at some point, they had to take the elevator to go to their rooms. I'd begin a conversation by introducing myself. "Hey, how's it going? I'm Louis Carr. What did you think of the sessions today?" *It worked every time.* We did the same thing throughout the years. Now, when I go to a convention, my presence is known.

The very relationships you establish can be leveraged to assist you in business. Here is how I transitioned out of an uncomfortable place:

- ◆ Introduce yourself with confidence. Be professional and authentic.

- ◆ In a concise manner, share what you do and what it is that differentiates you from your competition.

- ◆ Display integrity in your communication and behavior.

- ◆ Ask open-ended questions that allow people to talk about themselves.

- ◆ Be willing to serve others, whether that is offering to participate on a board or in an organization.

- ◆ Interact with people who possess good social skills. Take notice so you can learn from them.

- ◆ Do not insert yourself just to be present; engage so you can demonstrate your ability to listen, learn, and network.

- ◆ Leave an impression that allows you to stand out from everyone else.

- ◆ Once you acquire a business contact, have good follow-up.

———◆———

*Change and growth are an inevitable
part of our journey.*

———◆———

Sometimes people make the mistake of going to events to see what they can get out of it. Take the approach of determining what you can present and how you may be able to enhance someone's business or serve others. Once you make a connection, ask to get together and discuss ideas on how you can work together. It may take time to build a professional presence but if you do it appropriately, people will be interested in working to insert themselves into your network.

———◆———

*Sometimes people have to experience
different things to find their way.*

———◆———

- ◆ Before you make the decision to attend a networking function, identify your goal.

- ◆ Make sure the group, organization, or event you are attending is a professional representation of what you want to accomplish.

- ◆ The integrity and goals of the organization or people you network with should be aligned with yours.

When there are clubs, groups, events, or organizations that are not easily accessible or open to everyone, sometimes the people in that group or network don't know what they are missing. *Your goal is to insert yourself and show them.*

{ 13 }

SUCCESS IS A LIFESTYLE

Success: favorable or desired outcome

If you were to ask me if I had ever thought about being successful, I would answer yes; and then I could tell you when and why.

When I was a kid, my mother was consistent with putting me in situations that were uncomfortable. It was her way of helping me with my growth process. She had this thing, similar to "quiet time," that she called "thinking time." She would tell me to sit in a chair and think about how I was going to be successful, get good grades, be more disciplined, and then decide what I was willing to sacrifice. She would say, "You can't move, talk, or sleep. I just need you to think." So, I would sit there and think about how I was going to be successful. It didn't take long before my mother turned it into a routine, and it started to work.

In life, you set the tempo. You determine how fast you want to go by your willingness to put in the work.

At the age of twelve, I had my first real job working for my cousin. He had a newspaper and candy stand in the subway. My responsibility was to have the stand open and operating by five o'clock each morning. I was confident I could do the job since I had several exercises in "hard work" at home.

I would wake up by three, take a bus to the subway, and then a train to the newspaper stand. When I arrived, I would unbundle the newspapers, stack them up to make it easy for people to grab, bag up the apples and oranges, and then set up the candy and peanuts. Since my cousin had a fulltime job, I'd work the stand by myself, and he would check on me later in the day. At times, I was so sleepy that while I was making change for patrons, my head would start nodding. But I did that job all summer long without missing a beat.

This opportunity helped establish the behaviors that set me on the path of having a successful lifestyle by way of a good work ethic. In life, you set the tempo and determine how fast you want to go by your willingness to put in the work.

The problem with society today is that outside of sports, we don't want to push kids into an uncomfortable or challenging space. We act as though we don't want them to grow up. Most parents want their kids to remain kids as long as they possibly can—but it can hurt them from establishing those valuable behaviors early.

What I learned is that your behavior and everything you do must become a lifestyle based on being successful. If you are a good athlete, you want that to carry over to being a good student, as well as a good person. It does not mean that you cannot be a kid or that you have to be perfect, just be conscious of your behavior. Carry the same discipline and boundaries you have when you are on a team throughout your life.

———◆———

If you do not have discipline, you are like a leaf blowing down the street. You will end up anywhere.

———◆———

When I say *success is a lifestyle*, it is not in a material or monetary sense. I view it as a way of life spiritually, mentally, and physically. That is why I'm motivated to be healthy and fit. As I get older, I feel the need to protect that lifestyle. I don't want to be injured, sick, or feel that I can't do something any longer. In order to do my part to alleviate that scenario, I work toward maintaining the same level of fitness and endurance that I have always had. Yes, it hurts, but I am trying to set an example that it is possible to do whatever you want if you can commit to it. Success is a lifestyle, and your health is a significant part of it.

At the age of twenty-four, I went from my running weight of one hundred and eighty-five pounds to one hundred and fifty pounds. I could not eat anything I loved because it made me sick and caused considerable pain. Fearful that the diagnosis could be stomach cancer, I sought a doctor who could determine the cause of my symptoms. After seeing several doctors, it took a year and a half before I met a doctor who diagnosed me with ulcerative colitis, a chronic disease of the large intestine, also known as the colon. I found that years of happy but unhealthy eating had damaged my stomach and colon. The consequence was that I could no longer eat most of the foods I loved. He prescribed a course of treatment, which included steroids and a strict dietary regimen for almost two years.

My doctor and I became friends and he spent a great deal of time educating me about the illness. He told me most people don't heal from ulcerative colitis. He said, "It isn't because it is incurable, it's because they just don't have the discipline to change their lifestyle." If I wanted to change the course of my life and have more success with my prognosis, I had to change my lifestyle. The alternative was to deal with the pain and expect to be uncomfortable and frail. The pain was so bad that I remember thinking, if I could get out of that painful situation, I would never go back to eating the way I did. And I didn't. I followed the course of action, ate properly, drank a lot of water, and changed my entire diet.

By the age of thirty-two, my health was completely restored. If you don't take care of your health, your lifestyle will be disrupted. If you do not have discipline, you are like a leaf blowing down the street. You will end up anywhere. Take control of your life and understand that success has more to do with the overall quality of your life versus the quantity.

- ◆ Success encompasses your health, including what you eat, how you sleep, and your commitment to exercise. Good health is hard work, so start working on it early.

- ◆ Success is impacted by the individuals you allow in your circle of influence.

- ◆ Success is reflected in your ability to be organized.

- ◆ Success will expand with knowledge.

When you see great athletes and admire their skills, that is because they work at it, even when people are not watching. If you want to know if you are making progress, measure your overall emotional, mental, nutritional, and physical growth. If you cannot measure it, you are in the same place or losing ground. Each is an essential facet that requires attention throughout your journey.

If you want a successful lifestyle, understand what that means.

- ◆ You have to believe that success is for you. Not that it just exists and that it is possible, but that it is for you personally.

- ◆ Determine the path to get there.

- ◆ Even when you are not working on it, you have to remain focused. Everything you do has to be around your goal. It is a 360° plan.

- ◆ Do not accept or engage in negativity.

- ◆ Find mentors to give you guidance, assistance, or advice.

- ◆ Push yourself to do things you did not believe you could do.

Most successful people have a vision
that is bigger than themselves.

When you look at influential people like Steve Jobs, know their success depended on the engagement of others. He believed that his product would make our lives better and more efficient. When it comes to successful people, the common denominator is they have a vision bigger than themselves.

- ◆ They are all in, all the time, in a good way. They teach, mentor, observe every situation, and look for opportunities for others.

- ◆ They have a positive attitude. They can take the worst situations and find a silver lining.

- ◆ They have an understanding that it is not just about them. Their purpose is bigger than themselves.

{ 14 }

LEADERSHIP IS VISIBLE

Leadership: the power or ability to lead other people

When it comes to leadership, it is not for everyone.
Some people want to lead, but they do not know what it
takes to become a successful and respected leader. How
do you lead people from diverse backgrounds if you are
not acceptant of diversity? If you are not a subject-matter
expert, can you effectively advise people? If you do not
know or have limited interaction with your team, are you
able to motivate them? Is it possible to be effective if you
are void of a moral compass? To be an effective leader,
your team must trust and respect you and have confidence
in your overall decision-making.

Everyone has a starting point where they learn to
sharpen their skills. However, great leaders embark on

an endless journey, seeking education, training, and self-development.

- ◆ Leaders have vision to see beyond what is in front of them.

- ◆ Leaders display emotional intelligence and teach it.

- ◆ Leaders work comfortably in an uncomfortable place.

- ◆ Leaders know when to lead and when to trust others to lead.

- ◆ Leaders are inspirational and motivational mentors.

- ◆ Leaders are able and willing to serve others.

- ◆ Leaders establish great communication and comprehension with team members.

- ◆ Leaders know when to have patience, yet understand the importance of timelines.

- ◆ Leaders know when to stay the course and when to change course.

- ◆ Leaders know when to reinvent themselves and their environment.

Naturally, it is to your advantage to know someone's weaknesses but focus on their strengths. That will allow you to put them in a position to be successful. Determine how you can make that individual stronger and more confident. If it is a flaw and it needs to be corrected, find a way to help them.

———◆———

Leadership is exhibited by using your will, skill, and influence for the benefit of others.

———◆———

John H. Johnson established the definition of professionalism and firmly placed me on its path. He was a leader in every aspect and paid attention to the details. In my first interview with him, he noted my red shoes and the smallest flaw—a broken button on my shirtsleeve. Then, he told me I needed to move from the West Side of Chicago because I had not seen how big the world was. He gave me a direct lesson regarding the things I should learn because it was to the benefit of my career. Taking his advice could only make my journey a bit smoother.

Mr. Johnson was so engaged with his business that he could accurately anticipate things, which is a skill I learned from him. Great leaders should be able to see around the corner, and he could. He knew precisely what to expect from each person in his company. Nothing seemed to escape him. I never knew when Mr. Johnson would appear, but I could hear him coming because he wore a big chain on his belt that held his keys. I had tremendous respect for him because his leadership was visible and easily felt. He was present all the time and I learned that from him, too.

As an executive, I was responsible for selling advertising space. When I arrived at work, Mr. Johnson would be standing in the lobby of the building just to see if people were on time. At nine o'clock, he would get on the elevator and when the doors closed, we were late. One day, I saw him standing in the center of the elevator and the doors were beginning to *close a minute early*. I threw my brown briefcase into the elevator and jumped in. He said, "Don't just make it. Being on time means being early." He led by example, which was a warning of what he consistently expected of us.

Time management is a component of great leadership. When you are rushing to get things done, you are producing unnecessary stress. Learn to manage your ability to focus on your plan or vision. Then, have the discipline to follow it. When you do, you will have greater productivity.

John H. Johnson's image was larger than life. In 1982, he became the first African-American to appear on the *Forbes* 400, a list of the four hundred richest Americans. He was the wealthiest African-American in America. Mr. Johnson wore a suit and tie every day. His shoes were always polished and his hair stayed freshly cut. He had the perfect image for a business professional. As for his legacy, it was built from nothing. He was proud of his accomplishments and carried himself that way.

Mr. Johnson set the bar high in business. He wanted people to know that whatever needed to be done, we could do it because he had already done it. Organization was paramount. Whenever an order came in, it had to be reported to him immediately. He kept a little pocket-sized notebook that he wrote in daily. It was normal for him to ask, "Where are you going today?" and "What appointments do you have?" He was present and constantly challenged us to be on top of our business.

---

*Great leaders should be able
to see around the corner.*

Bob Johnson had tremendous energy and never appeared tired. He was always on and excited about all aspects of the business. I recall a time when there was a problem with the equipment in the conference room, but no one could fix it. Bob got up and fixed it. He knew everything about anything he was responsible for *on every level*. I never saw him any other way than all in and always on.

Bob built trust, which led to the sustainable relationships that he had in many fields. He had a way of educating and encouraging me while recognizing my commitment to his company.

We had executive retreats for our senior management, and Bob brought U.N. Ambassador Susan Rice to one of them. He surrounded himself with political people because he believed they had an international view of the world, which gave us a broader vision. Whenever he had the opportunity to teach us more, he did. When it came to knowledge, he had a wealth of information that he generously invested in us.

A great leader progresses and reinvents. Bob became a renaissance man and displayed diversity in his expertise. He was a lobbyist for the cable industry and then he became an owner. After he left the cable industry, he went on to participate in the hotel, automotive, and banking industries. Given he was a visionary, he wanted to be *first* in whatever he was going to do. A great leader is a great teacher that sets the bar high by example. A media magnate, Bob Johnson was the first African-American to become a billionaire. I consider Bob to be a great leader.

Being a leader means you are willing to consistently invest in yourself in order to be better for your team.

- Have vision. Learn to generate new ideas that can help bring about a paradigm shift.

- Learn how to identify the best talent for the role and environment.

- Base your leadership on having high morals.

- Learn to communicate effectively.

- Be persuasive and know how to construct con-sensus around a common goal.

- Lead by gaining the trust and confidence of others.

- Turn a good team into a great team.

- Make sure your activity is impactful.

- Be accountable.

- Develop a persona that people want to follow.

Both Bob Johnson and John H. Johnson took pride in creating opportunities to change lives. They both created monumental legacies.

{ 15 }

HOW TO BUILD
A GREAT BUSINESS TEAM

Great: remarkable in magnitude, degree, or effectiveness

Being a part of Lane Tech's track team is where I learned a valuable lesson about teamwork. To be effective and make an impact, you have to invest in getting to know your teammates, which has the ability to produce a remarkable, synergistic effect. Our team understood how one another thought and operated as individuals and we used that information to our advantage. Rather than allow injuries, personal situations, or anything to impede our progress, we worked right through them. Our focus was on the mechanics, speed, form, and timing. Once we accomplished that, it allowed us to deliver flawless handoffs of the baton on a consistent basis. Being on a great team meant that our focus was always on the same goal. Negative thoughts and egos were not a part of our mindset.

When it comes to a team, everyone has to be on the same page. It was clear that our coaches identified each of our strengths and then used them in the proper capacity in order to maximize our abilities and produce the desired outcome. Working and progressing in a culture fueled by motivation and focus was the only place we wanted to be.

———————◆———————

At the end of the day, great teams have their members on the same page all the time.

———————◆———————

When a team is not working together for a common goal or objective, things will fall apart. Your goals will not be achieved and, as a result, other problems may ensue. If you want to have success in business or any arena you step into, it is important to build a business team that can help you reach the overall goal.

Some NFL teams have a goal of a winning season. Only a select number have a goal of winning the Super Bowl. To be successful in either endeavor, they have to work toward the same objective. It happens in business, too. If you don't have a personal commitment or goal to win, you will not have the career you could have. Something has to drive you beyond where everyone else has been. Great teams are consistent and know what their team members are expected to do and will do all the time.

The number one thing that every great team wants to achieve is consistency, which is necessary in three key areas:

- Expectation
- Communication
- Execution

The way you achieve consistency is through practice. You see it in business, and in sports. It is evident in the environment, and the outcome will be reflected in the results.

How many times have people tried to teach you something beneficial to your overall growth or success, but you ignored their advice? Then, when a complete stranger gives you the same counsel, you respond as though you are hearing it for the first time, and receive it. Have you ever wondered why? It's because the advice does not have an emotional association.

Corporate environments can produce the same scenario. And just the same, an outside influence is precisely what is needed. They can help motivate, educate, or train your team to maximize productivity and efficiency while sharing in the accountability and results.

Theoretically, your team may be working hard, but not for the same goal. It is easy to assume that everyone is of the same mindset, but what happens when they are not? Some people may be working toward winning an award, advancing their career, or making money. Those are three different objectives. When that occurs, your team is not as strong as it should be.

Professional consultants are beneficial when it comes to presenting teams with the process of learning to work cohesively toward a common goal without disconnecting from it. Consultants have strategic benefits.

◆ They help you buy into a common mindset.

◆ They assist in defining goals and objectives.

◆ They give clarity around a team's strengths and weaknesses and help develop unique and effective solutions.

◆ Consultants can be a catalyst for change.

Train yourself to be a solution-oriented person, but be cognizant of the timeline.

If you have areas that need development, consider working with consultants. They can be effective contributors, assist with developing a strategy, determine effective ways to communicate, and motivate your team.

There is a process and formula to abide by, which will assist in building a great business team.

◆ Lay out objectives in a clear and succinct manner.

◆ Help your people acquire the will and skill to be successful. If they are not prepared emotionally and mentally, they will not be able to build a paradigm for success.

◆ Work with your team members on personal goals. If you get to know a person a little more than average, they will know you care.

◆ Be familiar with the habits of your team members. If you have someone working for you but you are not aware of their habits, whether they are good or bad, it can be a problem somewhere down the line.

◆ Be transparent; it removes doubt. Your team members must be able to trust you before they will follow you.

There is a myth that the higher you go, the easier it is. It is the exact opposite. The higher you go, the greater the responsibility.

When I became a manager, multiple management styles were not applicable to me because I treated everyone the same. I made the assumption that I could use one management style for everyone. I could either be hard, compassionate, or a driver. *I was a driver.* In time, I discovered that one management style was not effective. It was the same as taking a round peg and trying to force it into a square, triangle, or rectangular shape. It didn't work. I have since adopted and engaged multiple management styles that motivate people to achieve great expectations, goals, and results. The practice of multiple styles will sharpen your skills, team, and provide better results.

- ◆ To effectively lead people, become an expert on human behavior. Coaches do it all the time.

- ◆ Be able to read people quickly.

- ◆ Be knowledgeable about the industry, category, and business you are in.

- ◆ Be consistent in your behavior; people are always watching.

- ◆ Surround yourself with the best.

There is a myth that the higher you go, the easier it is. It is the exact opposite. The higher you go, the greater the responsibility. Great managers, like great coaches, use the things that are necessary to get the best out of people. You have to know what motivates, influences, and inspires someone to be the best they can be; then, adopt and use that particular management style.

It took many years of working with mentors and coaches, as well as studying successful people, to learn various styles and how to use them. It was a necessary part of my growth. I came to understand that all of the successful people I knew or read about had multiple styles to get the best out of individuals. You cannot motivate, inspire, or lead people unless you know them. I study people who work for me so I can learn how to activate the greatness in them.

{ 16 }

JOY KILLERS

Joy: success in doing, finding, or getting something

Most people want to be happy, but there are unavoidable situations that can cause happiness to fade at times. While the loss of a loved one, financial challenges, and health issues are plausible explanations, there are others that *are* avoidable. Life will always bring challenges but what you don't need is for a joy killer to bring them. Joy killers are people who operate to kill your spirit, and that is how they get their pleasure.

Just because you are happy does not mean everyone is happy for you. I found that out many years ago when a colleague of mine worked for someone who was all about killing joy. He said this man's entire vibe was ridden with negativity, and it seemed as though because he was unhappy, he wanted others to be, too. He would construct obstacles that would not only hurt people, but he was willing to sacrifice the business if it meant he could kill your joy. His time was deeply invested in strategically plotting to do things he knew would be upsetting and disruptive. Sadly, he routinely went to extremes to create negative situations for others.

My advice to my colleague was that joy killers lurk in every aspect of life. They can be anyone. They just don't want to see you successful or happy. They are intent on telling you what you cannot do, what is impossible, and what is not for you. They want to put you in a box and keep you there. The problem with joy killers is oftentimes they accomplish their goals.

Even when you have success, they will put a 'but' on it. People who give backhanded compliments and speak powerful words of negativity are everywhere. You are bound to meet some of those people, so don't absorb their negativity. If you do, it will only be a matter of time before you learn to be a joy killer, too.

As I advised my colleague, when you meet joy killers, use them in a positive capacity.

- ◆ Use them as motivation to go beyond what you believed you could do. That is what I have always done. Prove them wrong every single time.

- ◆ Do not keep them around any longer than necessary.

◆ Make sure you do not pick up any of their bad habits.

Joy killers do not have the final say when it comes to your happiness or destiny. Do not use them as an excuse as to why you didn't accomplish a goal or achieve the success you are destined to have.

{17}

AN INVESTMENT OF LOVE

Love: a feeling of strong or constant affection for a person

When someone makes an investment of love, you can feel it. My grandmother was the matriarch of our family and she made sure my mother and I knew how much she loved us. When the Korean War took her only son, her heart was broken. Once I was born, she loved me so much that my mother allowed my grandmother to raise me as her son, too. Since my mother had me at a young age, my grandmother helped guide her through the parenting process. In every aspect possible, my grandmother provided a feeling of security and love for both of us.

When someone loves you or cares about your well-being, they tend to have this proclivity to teach you things.

There was an immeasurable stream of wisdom that came from my grandmother. If I disagreed with my mother, I'd go right to my grandmother. She had a way of providing clarity as to why my mother made me do certain things. Ultimately, I could not do anything other than respect my mother's decisions. My grandmother taught me in her own loving way.

When it came to cooking, my grandmother was one of the greatest cooks around, and she was self-taught. She loved to cook and experience different things. The newspaper had a food column that provided recipes on a weekly basis. When the paper came, my grandmother would search for something new to try. And when she found something, she would cut out the recipe and make it. She was always filling the house with some form of love.

Get to know your kids. Understand where they are coming from and then shape and guide them along the way.

All of my friends respected my grandmother because of her compassion and ability to converse about anything, resolve issues, and relate to anyone. She carried herself in a way that demanded the respect she received. If any of my friends stopped by our home and I wasn't there, rather than leave, they would sit and talk with my grandmother.

When I came home late from a party, I would wake her up so I could tell her about it. But when Sunday came, my grandmother would wake me up and take me to church, which helped lay the foundation for my spiritual guidance. She was a contemporary, cool grandmother who listened and showed interest in me. I loved being around her. She was the polish around the rough edges. She taught me the value of money and even put my name on her savings account.

My mother always made sure I knew I was her son, but God blessed me because I had the best relationship with both of them. They made an investment of love that was without boundaries.

My grandmother's affection and engagement in my life had a tremendous impact. In hindsight, I learned my mother and grandmother were ahead of their time. They taught me values then, that were necessary for me to be successful today. My grandmother passed away from heart disease at the young age of sixty-five.

◆

Set expectations, have consistency, and make sure your children understand you care.

◆

It was a mild evening in October when I arrived home from work to the realization that my yard needed a bit of attention. Leaving on my blue and white checkered dress shirt, I quickly changed into a pair of gray sweatpants and slipped into my tennis shoes. I went back outside. Shortly after, my mother pulled up in her maroon Oldsmobile. After a few minutes, I noticed she had not gotten out. I wondered what she was doing, so I stopped the mower and went over to the car. She was crying.

"What is it? What happened?"

"Son," she began, "a mother spends a lifetime trying to develop her children and hope she's done a good job. I'm looking at the job that I've done, and I'm pleased."

"Okay, alright. Don't get sappy on me," I teased, watching my mother take in that particular moment of joy. I went back to cutting the grass and my mother finally went into the house.

That coming January, my mother passed away at the young age of fifty-five from heart disease. It was one of the greatest losses of my life. I was able to move her into a beautiful condo on Lake Shore Drive with an unobstructed view of the water. But the opportunity to achieve all of the things I wanted to do for her was lost because she was gone too soon. Her love, vision, and discipline kept me from going down any path but the one predestined for me. My mother never stopped watching over me.

I learned so much through that painful experience. When my mother passed, it hurt so much I cried every single day for three hundred and sixty-five days because the memory of her is extraordinarily strong. It didn't matter where I was or what I was doing, I couldn't control it. On the three hundred and sixty-fifth day, something happened. I had a physical reaction and coldness came over me. From that moment, every thought about my mother has been nothing but joy.

Although it came in hindsight, I realized my mother was ahead of her time. She had all these mental gymnastics that she made me do, and she would often tell me, "I have something for you, but I need you to share it." She had this initiative of teaching me to share. With consistency, regardless of where I was in life, she would remind me, "Don't get too high and mighty." My mother wanted me to be such a responsible man that she held herself accountable for my outcome. I was her number one priority. She worked on me to take care of myself so that I would be able to take care of my family. My mother executed on making sure that I received the lessons I needed and it was her desire, more than anything, *that I share them.*

By nature, we are a selfish people. The value of serving people is the lesson that is necessary to end selfishness.

{ 18 }

PREDESTINATION

Predestination: the doctrine that God in consequence of his foreknowledge of all events infallibly guides those who are destined for salvation

I believe in the power, vision, and protection of God. I believe in predestination. I have learned over the course of my life everything that happens to you is part of God's journey for you. The excitement is trying to figure it out. It's like a puzzle where you find little clues. Sometimes it says move to the next phase or go back to the beginning. The challenging part is when the clues are painful and the timing is different from your own.

If you don't have faith, it can impede your progress. We may not see it at the time, but the power that reflection has is purely educational.

Faith is hard because we do not know when answers or solutions are going to come, but the key is they will come.

Adversity is an unavoidable element of life that will change both you and your journey in some capacity. It creates the ability to have decisions, opportunities, and perspectives that you would not have otherwise. For example, attending Drake University would not have presented itself without my injury. I may not have believed in miracles without my injury. I was fired from Johnson Publishing and without that termination, I may not have ended up at BET. One of the greatest losses of my life is the loss of my mother, and I learned so much from that loss.

Some people do not believe there is anything more than what their current situation is because they choose not to see beyond that moment. Predestination does not mean that you can't change who you are or your current situation.

There are people who are at a disadvantage. However, they have neglected to realize hopelessness is a negative thought process as well as a choice. There are others who are disadvantaged, who do not accept that as their destiny.

Instead, through hard work, education, faith, and vision they change their circumstances.

Every situation we find ourselves in is a growth opportunity. It doesn't matter if it's negative or positive; it's what you choose to make of it. If someone tells you that you cannot do something, does that mean you should accept it? When I hear it, especially in regard to business, instinctively I question that type of negative thinking. It means they don't believe in me since they have already made a determination that I can't do something. What they don't know is I am one to prove that I can. My ability and destiny are not what someone says or believes it to be; it is what God has planned for me.

———◆———

Every situation we find ourselves in is a growth opportunity. It does not matter if it is negative or positive; it is what you choose to make of it.

———◆———

When I evaluate what has happened in my life, it is beyond human comprehension. If I tried to connect the pieces to grasp the entire picture, they would not fit. What I can tell you is, if you want to understand who you are, you must have faith to go on this journey. The learning process of understanding faith has taught me that when things are going wrong, God is omnipresent and that is when I am to be patient. Our test of faith lasts a lifetime. Faith seems to come when we are challenged, yet it should be present every day.

His ability to worship is a lifeline for him.

–Pastor Charles Jenkins

Having faith doesn't mean you don't do anything other than wait on God. While you are waiting, you should be doing something. If you don't know what that is, pray and ask what you should do. In the Bible, in every act of faith, Jesus told them to do something. Even though you are waiting, you still have to be active. It can be difficult when you are young and going through something. At that point, you have not heard all of the teachings and Scriptures from God that you need, and that is a good time to begin. At every level of my life, I understand the need for *faith* and *grace*. It is something that I lean heavily on for success. It allows me to have sustenance for my wife, work, and those I influence or impact in some way.

When I was a young adult, I didn't entirely understand how God transformed someone like me, who didn't have vision, to someone who has a lot of vision. But as the years passed, I realized it was predestined, and the core of predestination is faith. Regardless of what situation you are in, good or bad, you should understand this course or journey was decided for you long before your experience.

Let's not forget what God did for us two weeks ago, last year, or five years ago. Since life is constantly moving, we have the tendency to forget.

Things we may or may not expect are going to happen and they have taught me to have faith. Faith is an intricate part of my personal success, sanity, and ability to function. I view the worship experience and time in the Scriptures as both critical and pivotal to my ability to operate effectively on a day-to-day basis. When I attend service, it is as a student and not just as an attendee. I take notes because they provide clarity and understanding around the Scriptures. And when I feel obligated to share this knowledge with others, I do as a way of mentoring. Mentoring allows me to pass along the blessings that were given to me.

When you are faced with a challenge, rely on your faith. Instead of letting go or giving in, remind yourself, especially in difficult times, that you believe what you believe. At times, we have a short memory. Let's not forget what God did for us, two weeks ago, last year, or five years ago. Since life is constantly moving, we have the tendency to forget. We overlook the fact that we did not get ourselves out of previous situations. We think that we corrected the problems on our own. As a result, every time a difficult situation comes up, we forget the formula for success that resolved the previous issues.

Depending upon our journey, there are always twists in the road and things that we do not control. As we know, the loss of a loved one can throw us into an emotional whirlwind. Although it may not have been the first loss, it is easy to forget how we came through the situation before.

When it comes to your job, difficulties with resources or people will occur. If you have had a successful career, you have figured out how to get through it. But when it reoccurs, you may have that same emotional reaction. We tend not to use our past faith experiences to get us through, so we start all over again. Do not dismiss what your journey is teaching you; rely on it for better insight, wisdom, and clarity. *It has worked well for me.*

{ 19 }

EQUALLY YOKED

Yoked: to become joined or linked

People often say that opposites attract, and yes, that is true. But when they realize how much they don't have in common, the relationship becomes problematic, dysfunctional, or causes divorce. Having a successful marriage begins with being equally yoked.

When you choose a mate or spouse, it is necessary to have several things in common. You can anticipate there will be differences, but the core values that are important, in any type of relationship, must exist. When my mother met Diane, she said, "That one's sent from heaven." My mother had some kind of insight because she was right.

The secret to the success of my marriage is that my wife, Diane, and I share our core values. We have the same faith, we believe in God, and Christianity. We are supportive of one another in everything we do. Our work ethic is the same and so is our humor. We can be in the same room, but separated, and both of us will start laughing at the same thing because we are completely in tune with one another.

Having things in common, allows you to not only spend quality time together, but also understand one another's passion, drive, and commitment toward something. Naturally, there are things you won't necessarily have in common, and that's okay, too. Just respect them.

My wife is a thirty-year all-star in any wife-of-the-year contest. Her love, support, patience, and commitment have always been off the charts. I believe we have an advantage as a couple because we are equally yoked. It is important to have a capacity for caring and the ability to share.

Diane and I have interests that we don't necessarily share; however, we do not try to squash the other from doing them. Instead, we are supportive of one another's interests. For example, art is Diane's world, and she travels all over looking for a museum or gallery because she loves it. That's her thing and I support it one hundred percent. As for me, I'm into sports. I am the guy watching a couple of games on television, with a computer on my lap, and talking on the phone at the same time. It's what I do because it's what I love. But the beautiful thing about our marriage is that my wife never says anything that is not one hundred percent supportive of me. If I say that I am going to a game, her response is always favorable because she wants me to be happy and have fun. That is exactly what I want for her.

When you are happy in your relationship or marriage, it carries over into other relationships. My friends and family love my wife so much that I call her a "friend stealer." It's just amazing to me. I am constantly in awe of the way they are so into her and the way she is into them. She has this incredible energy and they love her because she has that "it" factor. People give her boundaries they would not give to anyone else.

When you are equally yoked, you do not have an unhealthy or competitive nature with one another. You do not waste time on little things that can become bigger. Your focus is on being happy. It is important to want the best for one another, personally and professionally, because you can feel it. That is a strong motivating factor when things become challenging.

The one thing I know for certain about my wife is that she wants me to be great. She is super proud of me and I hear it often. When I meet her friends, whether male or female, they say, "I know everything about you already." And when you know someone is completely in your corner, it makes you want to be supportive of that person in every way possible.

When it comes to having a successful marriage, those core values and beliefs act like conductors that facilitate a stronger connection. There are other areas to develop that can help you have a lasting marriage:

- Be in tune with that person from the beginning. It gives you wider boundaries and understanding.

- When you commit to someone, be in it to win it.

- Get to the stage where you no longer sweat the small stuff. Little bouts of negativity add up and become explosive.

- Make sure you understand and respect boundaries.

- It is important that you not only love your mate but that you *like* them. When you do, your tolerance will expand.

- Be happy with yourself and do not put the burden on your spouse to make you happy. Happiness begins from within.

When it comes to having a successful marriage, those core values and beliefs act like conductors that facilitate a stronger connection.

When you are committed to having a successful career in a constantly evolving industry, it is inevitable that it will be demanding. When you are focused on building or sustaining a career, the demand can cause a deficiency in other areas of your life, such as your relationship. That can produce stress. As we know, stress has a way of affecting everything, including your job. Make sure you go out of your way to remove it. Think about the relationship and what it needs before you allow it to fail. When you are equally yoked, you can see things coming that could be disruptive to your marriage and work together to prevent them.

In a marriage, the journey is not just for one, it is for both people.

My profession in the media industry causes me to travel extensively. I am completely dedicated to my career, so I do what is necessary. It is what I have done for over thirty years and I am passionate about the progress we have made.

Have you ever wondered if it is possible to sustain a happy and healthy marriage when your career is pulling you in multiple directions? Of course it is, when you know what to expect. Be transparent.

◆ Begin your relationship with open and honest communication about expectations and needs. Make sure to include dialogue about your career.

◆ Do not take a job without sharing what it involves with your spouse and family.

◆ Be mindful that after a challenging day, the expectations of your family are usually different from yours.

I have a dirty little secret. It has worked so well for my marriage that when I hire people who will be required to travel or work long hours, I ask them to do something. Get a *buy-in*. What a buy-in means is that your spouse, children, and everyone directly involved in your family dynamics need to understand what you will be doing and what it entails. They should be made aware that working long and hard is not a selfish thing because it benefits everyone in the family. After nearly thirty years of marriage, my career is still demanding, but because of the buy-in, it doesn't bother my wife. We have learned to successfully work around it. Initially, it may have been an adjustment; however, we both understood that it was a part of the process to build a successful career.

When you are able to send your kids to great schools, provide the things they want, and take them on vacations, give them an early lesson as to what your sacrifices and commitments are doing for them. It is important for you to be consistent with reminding them about the buy-in. Explain what your day or week consists of so they feel included in your life away from home.

When your day is over, make sure you arrive home with the same energy and passion that you invest in your career. Being home does not mean you shut down or turn off. And you should know this dirty little secret by now— you have to be *all in, all the time*!

At the end of the day, you want to bring balance to your *ask* for that buy-in. It is necessary to do things to reward your family for their sacrifices and understanding. Without a buy-in, you are going to have a lot of pressure that could have been avoided, so get the buy-in early.

In a marriage, the journey is not just for one, it is for both people. That is why my wife and I have consciously worked on setting and establishing dreams together. *I recommend it.*

{ 20 }

DIVERSITY

Diversity: the condition of having or being composed of differing elements

---

Even as the world continues to change and the "browning of America" progresses, diversity is still an intense topic for debate. In part, I attribute it to one's inability to value people from different backgrounds, cultures, and lifestyles. The problem begins with inception, as opposition to diversity will make it implausible to place value on those individuals.

During my career, it has been effortless for me to understand the value of diversity because I was exposed to its elements from high school through college. It was a fundamental part of my growth and journey. It produced a broader consideration, which I utilized throughout my career. However, I believe people of color have an advantage of understanding cultural diversity as it relates to others. In order to progress or be successful, most people of color must learn to operate outside of their own culture.

Over time, this debate on diversity has been perplexing. There is a consistent lack of urgency to comprehend or resolve issues, particularly when people say 'they get it,' yet remain in their ineffective holding position, averse to participating in a positive solution.

Employers persistently place blame on someone else by insisting qualified Hispanics, Asians, African Americans, women, and so forth are hard to find—as if they don't want jobs, opportunities, or to contribute. What is not being considered is that corporations and employers are doing themselves a disservice because they are not measuring what they are missing. They do not identify the contributions that would be of value by having diversity in employment.

Companies that provide products or services should understand what motivates diverse groups of people so they can effectively market to them. My preference is to continue learning from people who are different because their contribution, culture, and lifestyles facilitate having a better decision-making process.

There are viable opportunities for people to advance their experiences through diversity, which in return will improve their business. In observation of how rapidly demographics are changing worldwide, we should understand the benefit and want people who are a part of those demographics to be a part of the system.

We need to make sure that people value and appreciate our history, not what we have *been* through but what we have *come* through. That alone will help them understand that all things are possible.

I started The Louis Carr Internship Foundation to not only assist students of color but to help corporations take a look at America's future. I have invested my time and resources to help students have opportunities with major corporations and internship programs by way of giving back.

If your company and your vision are not looking like what America or the world looks like, you have a lot of work to do.

It is indefensible to make a claim that while job opportunities and internships are available, people of color are unavailable or unqualified; especially when corporations are located in major cities with a broad spectrum of a diverse population. Sometimes too much emphasis is placed on soliciting what they perceive as the "perfect candidate." Perhaps it is not the candidate that is wrong, but rather the perception of the perfect candidate.

Companies assume the perfect candidate is the individual with the exact experience over a precise time period. But perhaps the better candidate is that individual who has the basic fundamentals; is more committed, passionate, determined, and offers diversity.

People give too much attention to the position instead of the role that position plays on the team. When you think about sports teams, they recruit a franchise player and build around that person.

Businesses should take that approach as it produces the opportunity to have more flexibility in the type of positions and roles you are trying to fill around the franchise player. When I hire people, I don't just think about the role. I think about that role and its position as part of the team, which gives me more flexibility in deciding the type of person I need.

Bringing a diverse group of people together will take your management skills to the next level.

There is an overall culture that every company has. However, make certain the culture is flexible enough to respect, accept, and encourage differences. This will set you aside from everyone else. When people who are different are brought into an equation, allow them to be different. Do not make it mandatory to fit in. Allow people to contribute as themselves and you will more than likely receive their best contribution. This confidence displays more about the managers than the people.

Great managers, like great coaches, can manage people from different backgrounds with various personalities. Consider some of the sports teams that are comprised of people from all over the country or world. Their objective is to create a winning environment. How do winning coaches build successful franchises year after year with a cyclic progression of people from diverse backgrounds coming together? It happens when a coach has flexibility and understanding. Diversity begins with diverse thoughts. It is not only an issue of black and white; it encompasses race, age, gender, ethnicity, and personality. In a professional arena, my preference is to employ those who bring positive energy and challenge management to be at its best. We need corporate leaders who can create the type of acceptance and understanding that great head coaches possess.

Prepare your environment and yourself by expanding your boundaries.

Business owners must take the initiative to hire people who will expand and push management skills forward. Bringing a diverse group of people together will take your management skills to the next level. Management is about how you manage the people, process, and system toward common goals. If you routinely hire the same types of people, you have short-changed yourself and your ability to grow to be the best you can be. Focus on their contribution rather than worrying about the background. Understand you may have to manage them differently and protect them in a non-diverse environment. And that's okay because it is good for your business.

I believe if your company and your vision are not looking like what America or the world looks like, you have a lot of work to do.

{21}

ALL THINGS ARE POSSIBLE

Possible: able to be done

Life is a journey that will take us to some incredible places. Even though they may seem beyond our imagination and scope of comprehension, we will meet remarkable people and learn about the possibilities that exist. Our experiences will be comprised of challenges, lessons, and blessings that will help us with the growth process. The key is to sustain a willingness to learn and execute your vision with wisdom. Don't fight being special because, in time, you too will be ready to serve.

Over the years, there have been numerous individuals who have poured vision and knowledge into me. In doing so, they taught me some of their dirty little secrets about business and life in general. Instead of dismissing the advice or experiences they shared with me, I listened *and* learned from them. I have had countless hours filled with valuable debates, quick educational lessons, or passing of information, which has collectively contributed to my success. Once I began to learn, I began to evolve, and that evolution sparked my constant craving for knowledge.

Education is a key that can open many doors and show you a broader view of the world. It provides a foundation to build on so you can see the opportunities and possibilities that exist. I am in support of higher education because it allows you to aim higher for better opportunities. When I look in my rearview mirror, I can see how much I have learned and the value that education has brought to my success.

I believe I have an obligation to pass along what has helped me so that I can help others. *Dirty Little Secrets* is my way of teaching you what I have learned; so this information can benefit you at some point along your journey. We should be willing to pass along the things that have made us wiser, stronger, and better as individuals. Our goal should be to help one another succeed instead of celebrating one's failures. When you have the opportunity to mentor someone or teach them something, do it, just as others have done for you. And if you need to grow, find a mentor who can help you on a particular part of your journey. Their experiences and wisdom can keep you from making similar mistakes.

Each of us has someone who has given us something

to help us progress. When you see an opportunity to return that blessing, step up and be the difference in someone's life. Do the best you can and then mentor the next person.

As I put the pieces of my life together, the puzzle is still incomplete, but the vision is much clearer. My personal relationship with God has helped me understand that during my journey *all things are possible.*

It is important for me to be able to create as many successful people as I can. When it comes to winning, there has to be a purpose. People don't know why I am so driven because they don't know my purpose. It is for every person who was like me—didn't have a vision and grew up poor. I am trying to make sure there are enough soldiers to be able to carry on what I am doing.

APPENDIX

DIRTY LITTLE SECRETS

{1}

The time of 3:19:5 was a test of my will, skills, and commitment. You will have a time when you are tested, too.

{2}

Overcoming or defeating adversity depends on your mindset and your faith.

{3}

There will always be blessings and miracles. Appreciate and remember them.

{4}

Find your vision and execute it.

{5}

Regardless of your circumstances or where you are, God made you special in some way; so do not fight being special.

{6}

Hard work will help build a successful foundation. When you have to do it, do not be afraid of it.

{7}

Do not be afraid to go into that uncomfortable place. When you come out of it, you will be more confident and wiser.

{8}

Maturity is a journey of its own. Understand it is necessary and be willing to take it.

{9}

Take time to pray and understand your role in life.

{10}

If you want to stay current, learn to reinvent yourself. It is beneficial in life and business.

{ 11 }

Your image speaks; so be cognizant about what you are portraying.

{ 12 }

When it comes to your overall success in business, building a solid network of strong relationships is not only necessary, it is valuable.

{ 13 }

Success is not something you acquire and stop working for—it is a lifestyle.

{ 14 }

Teach by example because leadership is a visible thing.

{ 15 }

If you want to be successful in business, learn how to be a team player and build a great team.

{ 16 }

Beware of joy killers. They can only impede your progress and create a negative mindset, if you allow them.

{ 17 }

Recognize and appreciate the people who make an investment of love in you.

{ 18 }

Everything that happens with you is part of God's journey; so push through your challenges.

{ 19 }

When it comes to your relationship, make certain that the two of you are equally yoked.

{ 20 }

Learn to operate outside of your culture. Diversity has educational benefits that everyone can learn from.

{ 21 }

Even in the midst of adversity, hold onto your faith and remember that all things are possible.

ACKNOWLEDGMENTS

To the many people who have encouraged me to write this book, including my staff and so many personal friends, I couldn't have done it without your support.

To Kelli, who convinced me that the time was now or never, I thank you and your team so much.

Kevin, thank you for being there during every step of this journey. Without you, there wouldn't be a book.

To Phil, who opened a door that had been closed, I'll never forget it.

Charles, thank you for your clarity of God's Word.

To Marala and Alyssa, thank you for your expertise, guidance, and just making this fun. You're a big wow.

Finally, to all of the people who poured knowledge into me and saw something in me that I didn't see in myself. I am forever grateful.

ABOUT THE AUTHOR

Louis Carr, President of Black Entertainment Television Media Sales, is one of the most influential and prominent African Americans in the media and marketing industries. He has been responsible for more advertising dollars targeted toward the African-American consumer market than any other professional or company. He has been listed on NAMIC's Most Influential African Americans in the cable industry several times and received the Legend Award from Ad Color in 2013.

He has served on the boards of the Ad Council; International Radio and Television Society (IRTS); American Advertising Federation (AAF); and the Video Advertising Board (VAB), formerly the CAB.

He is a dedicated mentor and benevolent philanthropist. An advocate for diversity, Mr. Carr has hired more people of color and has the most diverse sales team than any other executive or company in the media industry. For more than twelve years, the Louis Carr Internship Foundation has dedicated its efforts to improve diversity in corporate America.

He currently serves on the board of the Boys Hope Girls Hope and the United States Track and Field Foundation. Mr. Carr resides in Chicago, Illinois, with his wife, Diane.

www.LouisCarrBook.com

www.LouisCarrFoundation.org

PURCHASE A COPY OF THE COMPANION BOOK BY LOUIS CARR:

Little Black Book